GW00630530

The Dons — In the League
has been published
in a Limited Edition
of which this is

Number 215

A list of subscribers
is printed at
the back of the book.

FRONT COVER: A classic action shot catches the ball the moment before it crosses the line for the fourth goal in a 5-0 win over Torquay United on Easter Monday 1979. Terry Eames (second right) took the corner, Ray Knowles (centre) flicked on and Tommy Cunningham headed home.

WIMBLEDON
FOOTBALL CLUB

THE DONS
– IN THE LEAGUE

The first five seasons 1977-1982

BY

STEPHEN JOHN CRABTREE

SPORTING & LEISURE PRESS
BUCKINGHAM, ENGLAND
MCMXCVI

PUBLISHED BY SPORTING & LEISURE PRESS
AND PRODUCED BY KEY COMPOSITION,
SOUTH MIDLANDS LITHOPLATES, CHENEY & SONS,
HILLMAN PRINTERS (FROME) & WBC BOOK MANUFACTURERS

ISBN 0 86023 558 0

CONTENTS

Manager Allen Batsford and his first captain Ian Cooke deep in thought.

Sources and Acknowledgements

My passion for Wimbledon FC began over 25 years ago and so I have witnessed first-hand many of the matches and incidents described in this book. However, it is only when you start reading about the past that you realise how fickle your memory can be. So I am indebted to a variety of local sports writers — particularly those from the *Wimbledon News* — on whose prose I have relied heavily (sometimes too heavily!).

Many people have commented on the text at various stages of production. Thanks therefore to go Peter Miller, Peter Cork, Ron Noades, Jennifer Crabtree and Richard Crabtree for their correction of factual errors and helpful advice. Reg Davis and David Barnard gave me support from within the Club and, without Paul Willatt's brilliant pictures, no book would have been possible. I am grateful to Allen Batsford as well, for agreeing to write the Foreword.

Hilary Procter's efficient typing made my task much easier as did Clive Birch and his team at Quotes Ltd, who approached the project with professionalism and enthusiasm.

Finally, thanks to my family — Kate, Sarah and Anna — for putting up with my obsession and encouraging me when my interest waned.

Dedication

For Sydney Black, the author's great uncle, whose dream it was to see his beloved Wimbledon in the Football League.

FOREWORD *BY ALLEN BATSFORD*

It is a great pleasure for me to write the foreword to this new account of Wimbledon Football Club. The book paints a vivid picture of the beginnings of the remarkable transformation which has turned The Dons from a football backwater to Premiership giants. It recalls in detail the final years as a non-League club and the early struggle to establish themselves in the Football League.

From a personal point of view I found memories came flooding back as I turned the pages: League titles, Cup Finals and those famous FA Cup-ties with Burnley, Leeds and Middlesbrough. It seems incredible that over twenty years have passed since those days as so many of the details remain vividly in my mind.

The real heroes were, of course, the players. I inherited a squad of only seven players when I arrived from Walton in 1974. I brought in others who quickly gelled into a formidable unit and we played most of that first season with a basic squad of only fourteen. The demands I made on them were tremendous but the spirit in the Club was superb. Three nights a week, after a full day at work, they trained under the main stand or in the car park. We played over sixty games a season, yet every time I asked for more effort they produced it.

Any good side needs leaders and I had four — Dave Bassett, Billy Edwards, Dave Donaldson and Ian Cooke. On the field they encouraged and moulded the others into a team. Roger Connell, the biggest hater of training I ever knew, always produced goals when it mattered and Dickie Guy, in goal, could be inspired by the big occasion.

The best moments? Going to Burnley, against a very well organised First Division outfit, and seeing our tactical plan work to perfection. Being applauded off the pitch at Leeds and Middlesbrough by generous local fans. And the day we finally got elected to the Football League.

There were moments of farce too. Our first Boxing Day fixture as a League Club was away to Rochdale. The coach company wanted to charge holiday rates, so we travelled up the motorway, like a pub team, in players' cars and lost 3-0. In Italy for an end of season tournament we were travelling back to the hotel by coach when suddenly the driver stopped and disappeared. We were left in the middle of nowhere without an interpreter or any officials with us. Eventually, after he had spent half an hour having a meal, he returned and drove on.

We stuck together whatever the situation and that has always been a feature of Wimbledon sides. I took great pride in the achievements of Dave Bassett as Wimbledon manager — his teams always had great spirit and a willingness to learn from their mistakes. As long as that remains the Club will continue to go from strength to strength. Enjoy the book!

Allen Batsford

INTRODUCTION

There is something unique about Wimbledon Football Club. How is it that a side with the crowd base of Chester City consistently succeeds in the Premiership? How can a team who sell all their best players win the FA Cup? What is the unique 'Crazy Gang' spirit which causes such loathing and respect?

Some believe that those who manage the Club must also have a way with loaves and fishes. Others have more down-to-earth explanations. Allen Batsford, the man who masterminded the successful side whch gained election to the Football League in 1977, says it's a case of the little man who has to fight for survival. For Bobby Gould, who led the Club to the FA Cup triumph in 1988, it's 'inner belief'. But Don Howe, who was Gould's assistant at the time, possibly gets closest of all. He says what is unique is a club where having the chairman and owner in on the half-time team talks is the most natural thing in the world.

Football is supposed to be becoming more Darwinian yet Wimbledon survive among the fittest, season after season. For the Premiership hierarchy the Dons are an anomaly who refuse to go away. For all the disadvantages posed by pathetic support, consequent lack of funds and the exodus of star players, the Club continues to survive, even thrive in the top flight.

Wimbledon have earned respect for their spirit and defiance if not their style of play and disciplinary record. The Club attracts enough column inches each season, both on and off the pitch, to make much 'bigger' clubs envious.

The players are nearly always overlooked until the consistency of the Club's record demands attention. The current players represent five different countries at international level. The list of former Dons, developed and then 'sold on', makes impressive reading – Beasant, Winterburn, Curle, Scales, Hodges, Wise and Fashanu among them. The rise of Warren Barton – from non-league to full international – underlines the way Wimbledon have maintained their record of unearthing talent.

The modern success story has its roots long ago, when the Club was neither respected or reviled, in the days when few people outside Wimbledon cared who they were playing. In the mid-1950s two men joined forces to begin Wimbledon's climb to the top of the English game. Sydney Black, a wealthy local property magnate, dreamed that one day his beloved Dons would compete with the best. He appointed Les Henley to take charge of his mid-table Isthmian League side.

Henley created a side which dominated the Isthmian League for a number of years before turning professional after the Amateur Cup win at Wembley in 1963. His team was immediately successful in their new Southern League surroundings and was among the top non-League outfits throughout the 1960s.

Black's death in 1967 broke the winning partnership and left the Club facing financial reality for the first time. After Henley was sacked in 1970 the side lost its way and different managers were employed, who failed in the face of inadequate resources and a lack of vision.

New Chairman Jack Beavan made his most inspired signing in June 1974 when he persuaded Allen Batsford to take over as manager. He brought with him from Walton a group of players who, in his words, 'had been through the mill'. Three successive Southern League titles, two headline-grabbing FA Cup runs and a place in Division Four soon followed. 'Apart from being good players they were experienced players, good leaders of men and we gelled,' Batsford said.

Once in the Football League, Batsford soon left, replaced by Dario Gradi with Dave Bassett, Batsford's combative Captain, as his assistant. By the time Bassett took over as manager in his own right in 1981 Sam Hammam had become the Club's owner and managing director.

Bobby Gould believes that the subsequent Wimbledon success story owes almost everything to the commitment of Hammam. 'Sam's passion for the game is incredible,' said Gould. His passion, together with the brilliance of manager Dave Bassett, turned an irrelevant little club from an unlikely corner of south-west London into members of the First Division by 1986.

They have remained there ever since, in spite of the upheaval of the move from Plough Lane to Selhurst Park and gates that average little over 10,000. In that time they have never mounted a serious Championship challenge or flirted with relegation. But one glorious afternoon in May 1988 Dave Beasant received the FA Cup from the Princess of Wales after a performance which left the nation stunned. If Sydney Black had been alive he would have been thrilled — his dream had come true.

This book is concerned with the period from August 1977 to May 1982. A time of learning and struggle, the team began the period in Division Four and ended up there again five years later. Seemingly little progress had been made but, behind the scenes, lessons had been absorbed which were the springboard for future triumphs. The innocent Club of 1977 had changed beyond recognition by 1982.

Allen Batsford's victorious Southern League side entered the Football League defiantly part-time. Their pre-season confidence quickly evaporated and gloom set in as the Club hovered close to re-election places by Christmas. Disagreements between Chairman Ron Noades and Batsford led to the latter's departure in the early days of 1978.

New boss Dario Gradi quickly turned the Club into a full-time outfit and swept away the non-League outlook. The Club was mid-table by the end of the season and unbeaten for thirteen matches at the start of the next. Despite a few hiccups, promotion followed and Division Three was reached.

1979-80 was a difficult season with a young, enthusiastic side proving too naive for the higher sphere. Lack of finance due to poor attendances caused problems and Noades began to question how far he could develop the Club.

By Christmas 1980 his frustration was clear and he had initial talks with Milton Keynes Development Corporation. His aim was to move the whole Club to a place where there would be little local competition for support, and space to build a multi-purpose stadium. Instead, by February he had bought a controlling interest in Crystal Palace and planned that both clubs should share Selhurst Park.

A vocal campaign caused him to relent and allow his shares in Wimbledon to be sold. The major purchaser was Sam Hammam and, with Gradi moving to manage Palace, Bassett became boss at Plough Lane.

An incredible run of twenty-one games with only one defeat in the early months of 1981 ensured another promotion for the Dons. Once again the team was not ready for its elevation and the yo-yo existence continued as they were relegated on goal difference in May 1982 despite a brilliant late run.

This time lessons had been learned; the management duo of Hammam and Bassett proved to be an inspired double act. The Club had a crop of young talent that was ready to take the football world by storm.

Much credit should to go Ron Noades. Much reviled by modern Wimbledon supporters, it was he who transformed a ramshackle behind-the-scenes organisation into a professional, profit-making club. He also campagined tirelessly for that Football League place. On the eve of the first League match versus Halifax Town he revealed the Club had a ten year plan to reach Division One. The experts ridiculed him as hopelessly ambitious.

In fact Noades over-estimated the time needed to reach the top. Ironically it was his departure in 1981 which proved the catalyst for the remarkable ascent. Into the vacuum stepped Sam Hammam, with his unique combination of passion, hard work and shrewdness. The Club has not looked back since.

ABOVE: Pat Edelston, who scored 35 goals in the 1946-47 season, just fails to connect with a cross at Highbury in the 1947 FA Amateur Cup Final. BELOW: Eddie Reynolds (far left) heads the first of his four goals against Sutton United in the 1963 FA Amateur Cup Final at Wembley.

The Non-League Years

1889-1974: A brief look

Wimbledon Football Club was born well over one hundred years ago. Something of a late developer compared to many teams, they spent nearly nine decades playing their football outside the Football League before their elevation in 1977. The beginnings were inauspicious. The Club was formed by a group of old boys from the Central School on Wimbledon Common. It was 1889 when Wimbledon Old Centrals played their first match, close to Robin Hood Road, and beat Westminster 1-0. The Club colours were navy blue and white and the teams changted at the nearby Fox and Grapes.

By 1896 the 'Old Centrals' had begun winning trophies — the Clapham League and Herald Cup. The League was won twice more before the Club obtained its first private ground, near Raynes Park Station, 1901.

In 1905 the members voted to change the name to 'Wimbledon F.C.'. The new name obviously helped, as the team won the Mid-Surrey League in 1905-6 — their first year in the competition. Until the First World War, the Club used a succession of grounds in the Wimbledon area as they struggled financially. Then, just before the war began, the Dons moved to Plough Lane, which was a patch of swampland used as a refuse tip.

For two years after the war Wimbledon competed in the Athenian League before being elected to the Isthmian League in 1921-2. Throughout the 1920s the Dons struggled to establish themselves in the country's top amateur league. But the hard work eventually paid off when Wimbledon became League Champions in successive seasons in 1930-1 and 1931-2. The financial bonanza generated by success enabled the Plough Lane ground to be considerably developed.

It was 1934-5 before the Dons were Champions again, in a season in which they also reached the FA Cup 2nd Round proper and the final of the Amateur Cup. That final against Bishop Auckland ended in a 0-0 draw in front of 20,000 at Ayresome Park, then Wimbledon lost the replay 2-1 with 32,000 people inside Stamford Bridge.

Another Championship followed the next year but, until the outbreak of the Second World War, the Club had to be content with mid-table league placings. Plough Lane suffered extensive damage during the hostilities and, as the 1945-6 season opened, there were problems both on the financial and playing fronts. Nonetheless, hard work, on and off the pitch, led to the Dons reaching the Amateur Cup Final of 1947. That attracted 47,000 to Highbury as Leytonstone ran out winners by two goals to one.

In the Isthmian League the Club's progress was less spectacular with the Dons failing to win the Championship between 1946 and 1958. However, during this period, under the guidance of Chairman Sydney Black, the ground was developed into one of the finest stadiums outside the Football League.

In the summer of 1956 the Management Committee decided to appoint Les Henley as Club coach for the following season after three disappointing years. His method slowly took effect with the Dons finishing 13th, then 7th and finally, Champions in the 1958-59 season. The team finished six points clear of Dulwich Hamlet and were unbeaten at home. A local derby with Tooting and Mitcham attracted 6,946 to Plough Lane.

The next two years saw Wimbledon finish third in the Isthmian League before the Championship returned to SW19 in 1961-2 and 1962-3. The latter season saw the

Dons beat a Football League side for the first time — Colchester United in the FA Cup — and then finally win the Amateur Cup. Over 45,000 people saw Sutton United beaten 4-2 with all the Dons' goals coming from the head of Eddie Reynolds — a unique feat at Wembley.

A hat-trick of Isthmian League titles was completed in 1963-64 before the Club took the momentous decision to turn professional. They applied to join the Southern League and were duly elected and joined the 1st Division for the 1964-5 season. The Dons were promoted immediately, by finishing runners-up to Hereford United, who joined them in the Premier League.

Still managed by Les Henley, Wimbledon adapted quickly to life in a higher sphere, finishing successively 5th, 4th, 2nd, 3rd, 5th and then 9th in the Southern League Premier Division. The only silverware obtained during these years was the Southern League Cup in 1969-70 but the Dons were proud of their position among the elite of non-League clubs.

The death of Chairman Sydney Black in 1967 meant that the Club could no longer rely on a financial benefactor. When Les Henley was sacked as manager at the end of the 1970-1 season the Dons' fortunes slumped alarmingly. The Board wanted a young player-manager in charge on the field and appointed Mike Everitt. Despite topping the table in October the Dons slumped into the bottom half after Christmas and only a late revival ensured 10th place. Wimbledon also had the dubious distinction of being eliminated from all four Cup competitions at the first hurdle.

Despite some improvement in their Cup fortunes the Dons could only finish 12th in the League in 1972-3. It was clear that Everitt's side was not going to win any honours and crowds began to fall off. For the first time gates failed to reach 1,000 and the financial position worsened.

On the Monday before the 1973-4 season began it was announced that Mike Everitt had quit to become manager of Brentford. Within a week, despite rumours of the return of Henley, Dick Graham, the ex-Colchester boss, was appointed. Chairman Jack Beavan said of his new manager 'We wanted a man with experience and contacts and we have got just that'.

Graham's first game in charge was a 5-2 win over Weymouth — an encouraging start. However, injuries to key players and a worrying lack of commitment from the rest of the team led to some poor results and a slide down the table. The month of March was a disaster and ended Graham's short time at the helm. Five matches produced five defeats, leaving the team in 18th place and facing relegation. The last in a series of disputes between the Board and Manager led to the latter's resignation at the end of the month.

Trainer Danny Keenan and the senior players took over training and team selection and a new spirit was forged. The last ten games produced fourteen points and the Dons finished in a comfortable twelfth place. Nonetheless, with only seven players retained, no manager and little money to attract new men, the future looked bleak.

The Supporters' Club Secretary Ken Chaplin looked forward to the 1974-5 season as he wrote in the Clubs' handbook: 'This will have been our tenth season in the Southern League and apart from one Cup success and two runner-up league placings we have achieved very little in nine seasons. We have gone through these depressive periods before and a saviour has always been found. Now more than ever we need another saviour, to get Wimbledon back to its pinnacle of success'.

A saviour was found; his name was Allen Batsford.

ABOVE: Wimbledon players celebrate winning the 1963 FA Amateur Cup Final at Wembley. BELOW: Gerry O'Rourke threatens the Bristol Rovers goal during an FA Cup-tie in January 1968.

ABOVE: Players and supporters observe a minute's silence, before the game against Cambridge United in April 1968, as a mark of respect for Sydney Black, who died that week. BELOW: Player-manager Mike Everitt in action at Cambridge City.

1974-75: An amazing year

Allen Batsford took over Wimbledon in the summer of 1974 after seven successful years at Walton and Hersham, but such was the financial situation he almost did not have a Club to manage. During the week he was appointed £5,000 was found — £2,500 from the Supporter's Club and £2,500 from Club President Bernie Coleman — to prevent the bank closing down the Dons.

Former Arsenal man Batsford was cautious as he reflected on the task ahead: 'The Wimbledon job became vacant, it offered me a challenge and I'm happy to take it up. I wouldn't be coming to Wimbledon if I didn't think I could do a good job'.

The size of that challenge was made clear when he discovered that only seven men had been retained from the 1973-4 season, namely Dickie Guy, Bob Stockley, Dave Lucas, Ian Cooke, Selwyn Rice, Mick Mahon and Jeff Bryant. It was fortunate that all were excellent players, as the Board then informed him that they could only afford £15 per week for each new player he signed, and there was no cash for transfers or signing-on fees.

Batsford quickly brought five players who had previously worked with him to Plough Lane. Defenders Dave Donaldson and Billy Edwards, mid-field man Dave Bassett and strikers Roger Connell and Kieron Somers had all appeared for Walton in the Amateur Cup Final of 1973. It was these five, plus the seven retained men, who formed a team which rocked the football world in 1974-5.

After losing 2-0 at Nuneaton Borough on the opening day of the season, the Dons then won an amazing 22 matches in a row. Of these, eleven were League games and eleven were Cup ties. The Dons had entered four different Cup competitions and their early successes meant that Southern League matches were simply squeezed out.

The 21st win in the sequence came agains Bath City in the FA Cup 1st Round proper — a competition in which Wimbledon had already completed four ties. An exciting match was settled by a brilliant long-range drive by winger Mick Mahon, his injury time winner watched by over 5,000 people. So the Dons ended November still in four Cup competitions and third in the League despite having played so few games.

The table looked like this:

	P	W	D	L	F	A	Pts
1 Yeovil Town	18	12	2	4	35	16	26
2 Nuneaton Boro'	16	11	2	3	26	15	24
3 WIMBLEDON	12	11	0	1	28	8	22
4 Kettering Town	17	9	2	6	32	21	20

The winning run ended at Cambridge City — Edwards scored in a 1-1 draw — but another home FA Cup win soon followed, to put the side through to a 3rd Round tie away to 1st Division Burnley. That Cup win, 2-0 over Kettering, was followed by five League games in eighteen days before travelling north. Of these two were won and two were lost as fatigue showed for the first time.

At Turf Moor the Dons became the first non-League side to win at a 1st Division club's ground for 52 years. Mick Mahon's 49th minute goal put paid to the Claret's hopes, in a match which went down as one of the biggest shocks in FA Cup history. The whole team battled brilliantly and Dickie Guy, in goal, made three unbelievable saves.

Afterwards an overjoyed Allen Batsford commented: 'It all worked out exactly as we planned it. I feel sorry for Burnley but this was a great day for us. We deserved to win and I am proud of every member of our side. The last 20 minutes were sheer hell for me, but Guy was magnificent'.

The 4th Round draw paired Wimbledon with reigning champions Leeds United. An Elland Road full house of 46,000 saw the Dons continue to confound the critics by forcing a 0-0 draw. Once again Guy was the hero. His 82nd minute penalty stop from Peter Lorimer ensured he dominated the back pages of the Sunday papers. The fact that the match was televised ensured national fame for the team and Guy in particular.

The replay, due to take place at Plough Lane three days later, was postponed due to a waterlogged pitch and was then switched to Selhurst Park on police advice. Such was the interest in the tie that 45,000 turned out to see Wimbledon edged out by a deflected Johnny Giles goal. The man who turned Giles' shot past a despairing Guy was Dave Bassett who afterwards defended the team's defensive approach: 'I know we could have pinched a goal in the opening minutes but if we had tried to attack them they would have slaughtered us. They have so much skill, speed, fitness and talent'.

So it was back to non-League business. Under two weeks after the Leeds defeat the Dons re-established themselves as favourites for the FA Trophy by walloping Telford 4-1 in the 3rd Round. The competition offered another route to Wembley but a 1-0 defeat at Scarborough in the quarter-finals ended Wimbledon's hopes. The following Monday they crashed out of the Southern League Cup at Kettering leaving only the London Senior Cup and the championship to aim at.

On 15 March Dagenham came to Plough Lane to grab a replay following a 1-1 draw in the London Senior Cup semi-final. At the Victoria Ground the Dons rediscovered their form, winning 2-1, to set up a final with Leatherhead at Dulwich Hamlet's ground. In front of over 3,000 fans at Champion Hill two brilliant Ian Cooke goals brought the Cup to Plough Lane for the first time.

There were still nine League matches to play in just eighteen days and remarkably, thirteen points were obtained by an exhausted team. The Dons' first Southern League Championship was clinched following a 1-1 home draw with Telford on 1 May. The season finished the next day with a 2-0 win at Atherstone, leaving a final record for the season of Played, 73, Won 49, Drawn 10, Lost 14, for 128 and against 52.

All this was achieved with a basic squad of 14 and one of those, reserve goalkeeper Paul Priddy, played only one game. The team's success was based on a solid defence with Dickie Guy in goal, Jeff Bryant and Dave Donaldson a brilliant pair of centre backs and Bob Stockley and Billy Edwards at right and left back respectively. The midfield normally comprised the tough tackling Dave Bassett and Selwyn Rice, supported by Player of the Year Ian Cooke. Up front, winger Mick Mahon supplied crosses for Roger Connell and Kieron Somers, who scored over 60 goals between them.

After all their success the Dons sought election to the Fourth Division at the Football League AGM in June. But the League Chairmen were not impressed, voting back all of their current members, leaving the Dons with only four votes. Disappointed Allen Batsford commented after the meeting: 'We must build ourselves up into the best non-League side in the country so they cannot ignore us. There are a few areas where we can improve, such as administration, and we need a bigger playing squad'.

The proposed Alliance League — a division made up of the top clubs from the Southern and Northern Premier — offered a crumb of comfort for disgruntled Dons fans. It would create the possibility of a 'Fifth Division' with automatic promotion and relegation. But all this was in the future as Wimbledon prepared for more success in the 1975-6 season.

ABOVE: Mick Mahon (centre, light shirt) scores the winner at Turf Moor in January 1975. The grounded Roger Connell looks on admiringly. BELOW: Ian Cooke beats Frank Grey and Gordon McQueen at Elland Road in the FA Cup 4th Round tie.

ABOVE: Kieron Somers (far left) can only glance and Roger Connell (far right) cannot look as Dickie Guy saves Peter Lorimer's weak kick at Leeds. BELOW: Despair for Guy as Giles' shot has just deflected past him at Selhurst Park in the 4th round replay.

ABOVE: Skipper Ian Cooke collects the Southern League Championship Shield from League President Jim Parrish at the end of the 1974-75 season. BELOW: Plough Lane, the home of Wimbledon FC since 1912, in its pre-league days. Picture taken from the Wandle End looking towards the West Bank.

ABOVE: Ian Cooke receives the Northern Premier v Southern Premier Champions Cup after the defeat of Wigan in November 1975. BELOW: The victorious Dons display the Southern League Cup after the defeat of Yeovil Town in April 1976. The players (from left) are Tilley, Bassett, Rice, Bryant, Donaldson, Holmes, Connell, Guy, Cooke, Leslie and Edwards.

1975-76: A League and Cup double

By 1975-6 Wimbledon had become the side everyone wanted to beat and it was clear that repeating the exploits of the previous season would be difficult. Right back Bob Stockley departed during the summer for Atherstone, and was replaced by Henry Falconer. The only other recruits were ex-Wrexham mid-fielder Tommy Vansittart and striker Billy Homes from Barnet.

Despite the changes, after an opening day draw at Cambridge City, the Dons won eight consecutive League games to be top of the table by the end of September. The early rounds of the Southern League Cup competition proved equally successful, with wins against Hillingdon Borough and Romford. As Champions, Wimbledon took part in the Southern League Championship match, beating Kettering 1-0, and the Northern Premier v Southern Premier Champions Trophy, defeating Wigan over two legs.

The Dons made progress in the various other Cups throughout October and November. Finchley were despatched in the London Senior Cup while Kingstonian returned home on the wrong side of a 6-1 scoreline in the FA Cup. In the League, defeats at Atherstone and Dunstable, combined with a 2-0 home reverse against Bath, made their top-of-the-table position look less secure. At the end of November the table was as follows:

	P	W	D	L	F	A	Pts
1 WIMBLEDON	16	10	3	3	24	11	23
2 Nuneaton Boro'	14	7	7	0	16	7	21
3 Dunstable Town	15	10	1	4	26	13	21
4 Maidstone United	16	7	7	2	22	14	21

With fixture problems looming, Wimbledon contrived to make things worse with consecutive home Cup draws against Chelmsford and Enfield in the Southern League and London Senior Cup respectively. However, an excellent FA Cup win at Nuneaton set up an attractive local derby at home to Fourth Division Brentford. Nearly 9,000 fans, the biggest home crowd for seven years, saw the Bees win 2-0. Ironically it was an inspired display by Paul Priddy, who had moved to Griffin Park after being frustrated by the lack of opportunities at Wimbledon, which kept out the Dons' attack.

To cap a disastrous day, manager Allen Batsford was cautioned along with skipper Dave Bassett. Both went into referee Nippard's notebook for dissent and Bassett was furious afterwards. He dismissed his booking for alleged dissent at a throw-in and added: 'We should have had a penalty when I was brought down in the closing stages but he blew for time'.

Two days before Christmas Wimbledon were dumped out of the London Senior Cup as well, beaten in a replay at Enfield. There was no respite as 1976 opened with tough away trips, within three days, to Kettering and title rivals Nuneaton Borough. On New Year's Day nearly 3,000 at Kettering's Rockingham Road ground saw the Dons fight back from 2-0 down for a 3-3 draw. While at Nuneaton, John Leslie was stretchered off and Kevin Tilley was sent off as Wimbledon slumped to a 1-0 defeat.

Down to 4th place in the League, Wimbledon continued to make progress in the remaining two Cup competitions. They overcame Sutton in the FA Trophy after a replay, and Chelmsford in the Southern League Cup after two replays. But January ended with a disappointing 0-0 draw at home to Dagenham in the FA Trophy. The replay, three days later, ended any hopes of a trip to Wembley as the Dons slipped to a 2-0 defeat.

The target ahead was now clear — a Southern League and Cup double. The defeat of Burton and Dover put the Dons through to the final of the Cup competition, while wins at Bath and Yeovil strengthened their League position. The number of Cup-ties had left the side once again with games in hand but little time to play them. With two months of the season to go there were twenty fixtures to be played and a League table that looked like this:

	P	W	D	L	F	A	Pts
1 Dunstable Town	30	16	5	9	49	30	37
2 Maidstone United	30	12	13	5	40	28	37
3 Yeovil Town	28	12	10	6	31	35	34
4 WIMBLEDON	24	14	5	5	35	18	33
5 Nuneaton Boro'	27	10	13	4	23	21	33

Throughout March, Wimbledon continued to play well and a crucial 3-0 home win against leaders Dunstable edged them nearer the title. A week later at Stourbridge, young John Leslie, a signing from Dulwich Hamlet, scored four times in a 6-0 win, only to be dropped three days later as Mick Mahon retuned from injury.

The Southern League Cup-final was a two-legged affair. The first game at Yeovil was a tense occasion and a Billy Holmes penalty ensured the Dons returned to London all square. At Plough Lane an own goal and an Ian Cooke header won the Cup, despite an injury time strike from Yeovil's Plumb.

With six League matches still to go, Wimbledon needed several more wins to ensure their second successive title. Any nervous supporters need not have worried, as their favourites stormed home with five wins and a draw to finish eight points clear of second-placed Yeovil Town.

The last home game proved highly controversial as referee Mike Taylor dismissed six players — three from each side. Matches with Wealdstone had proved fiery in the past and this was no exception. Ironically, before the Dons' 4-1 win, the Southern League Championship Trophy had been presented. 'We did some silly things out there', admitted Batsford. 'It's a very sad night for the Club and I have no quarrel with the sending offs.'

Due to their status as one of the top non-League sides in the country, Wimbledon were invited to take part in an end of season tournament — the semi-professional Anglo-Italian Cup. The two home games in their group — against Benevento and Siracusa — provided easy victories, as the Dons won 4-0 and 3-0 respectively.

On the eve of flying to Italy for the return games, Wimbledon received just three votes at the Football League's AGM. Yeovil managed the highest number of non-League votes with eighteen as Stockport, Newport, Southport and Workington were all re-elected. Batsford was realistic as he said: 'Yeovil have been campainging solid for three months, we haven't done enough. We must work harder'. It was a mistake that would be rectified twelve months later.

Once in Italy, Wimbledon experienced some tough tackling in their games, leading Batsford to comment memorably: 'We were kicked from one end of Italy to the other'.

A 1-1 draw at Benevento and a defeat by 1-0 to Siracusa were still enough for Dons to reach the final as the top English side. The refereeing in the final against Monza can best be described as 'controversial' as Wimbledon lost 1-0. One Italian player appeared to be booked twice but was not sent off.

So the season did not end until late June, leaving a short close season, and the Dons declined future offers to take part in the tournament. Their eyes were set firmly on a Football League place but, to achieve it, the organisation off-field would have to match the brilliance on it. A new, and more ruthless Chairman was needed.

ABOVE: Roger Connell flicks the ball over Middlesboro' 'keeper Cuff as Marlowe, Edwards and Cooke close in. BELOW: John Leslie (far right) has just scored the vital first goal against Kettering in April 1977. Edwards and Cooke join in the celebrations.

ABOVE: Tony Greig joined the Wimbledon board as the campaign to join the league picked up strength. Greig (second left) is joined by Jimmy Rose, Allen Batsford, Ron Noades, John Reed and Bernie Coleman. BELOW: Champions for the third time. The 1976-77 team face the camera. Back row: (from left) Rice, Edwards, Marlowe, Eames, Bryant, Markham, Guy, Donaldson, Leslie, Aitken. Front row: Bassett, Tilley, Holmes, Batsford, Cooke, O'Brien, Connell.

1976-77: Into the League at last

Despite being Champions for the second year running, Wimbledon had managed to turn a 1975 profit of £35,000 into a deficit of £20,000 by 1976. Change behind the scenes was badly needed and it came with the arrival of 39-year-old Ron Noades as Chairman. Initially the players were offered the chance to run the Club on a co-operative basis by chief shareholder, Bernie Coleman. They declined and, despite a substantial offer from QPR Chairman Jim Gregory, who wanted Plough Lane as a training ground, Coleman sold the Club to Noades, who he felt would run it for the benefit of Wimbledon.

Noades, a property developer, had transformed Southall, his previous Club, both on and off the pitch. Within two years as Chairman he had put them back in the black financially and watched the side gain promotion. Together with Jimmy Rose, Noades guaranteed the debts and began the task of making the Club financially solvent. Further generosity from Bernie Coleman helped. He donated the Sportsman public house to the Club, which was to provide substantial income down the years.

Meanwhile Allen Batsford was trying to sign new players to replace those who had moved on — Mick Mahon, Tommy Vansittart, Henry Falconer and Kieron Somers. Before the season began he managed to persuade Kevin Tilley, Leo Markham and Ricky Marlowe to join, but Southall turned down a £5,000 bid for Alan Devonshire. The tricky winger was later to star for England and West Ham in an illustrious career.

It was an unfamiliar Dons side that took the field for the opening match of the season; a Southern League Cup-tie at Romford. No less than six players were suspended; Aitken, Rice and Leslie were out for three matches following the April match with Wealdstone while Bryant, Connell and Cooke had to miss one match following cautions in the Anglo-Italian tournament. The situation was so bad that Wimbledon had no substitutes and matters were made worse when Billy Holmes was sent off in the first half at Brooklands as the Dons crashed to a 2-0 defeat.

With the side regaining a more familiar look the Dons hit back in the second leg at Plough Lane. A goal four minutes from time, scored by Roger Connell, ensured a 2-0 win which forced a replay. But the League campaign also opened poorly with no goals and only one point from their first three matches.

Gradually Wimbledon returned to form as September progressed. They won four successive home League games as well as on visits to Weymouth and to Romford for the Cup replay. However, they were clearly not back to their best form, as October included defeats by Yeovil in the Championship match and Bath at home in the League. Lowly Walthamstow Avenue were only dispatched from the London Senior Cup after a replay and 1st Division Barnet won a Southern League Cup replay at Plough Lane.

After beating Margate 2-1 on 6 November, Wimbledon were in fifth place with thirteen points from eleven games.

	P	W	D	L	F	A	Pts
1 Kettering Town	12	5	7	0	18	8	17
2 Bath City	11	6	4	1	13	6	16
3 Telford United	11	8	0	3	17	10	16
4 Reddich United	9	6	3	0	19	6	15
5 WIMBLEDON	11	6	1	4	16	11	13

The FA Cup seemed to spark the Dons into life as they rediscovered some of their old form. Over 2,000 people were at Plough Lane to see Wimbledon beat Woking in the First Round with a single Connell goal. The home side were kept in the tie by some brilliant goalkeeping by Dickie Guy, making his 500th appearance for the Club.

Ten days later Wimbledon produced their best display of the season at Runcorn's Canal Street ground, winning 3-1 (aggregate 3-2) to retain the Northern Premier/Southern Premier Champions Trophy. The reward for beating Woking was a 2nd Round trip to Leatherhead. After rain had caused the match to be postponed, on the Saturday two Ricky Marlowe goals helped the Dons to another 3-1 win in front of over 4,000 at tiny Fetcham Grove.

Before the Third Round tie with Middlesbrough, Wimbledon won three successive League matches without conceding a goal, leaving them five points behind the leaders with games in hand. Jack Charlton's dour Boro' side attracted only 8,000 to Plough Lane for a hard-fought 0-0 draw. Afterwards Wimbledon were unhappy with the 1st Division side's aggressive tactics, while Charlton thought the Dons had deliberately churned up the pitch.

Goalkeeper Guy was at his best once again in the replay, superbly marshalling his defence on a dangerous snow-covered surface. Only a David Armstrong penalty beat him, as Wimbledon won the plaudits of the 23,000 crowd. Three days later the FA Trophy campaign began with an excellent 1-0 win at Grantham. The prospect of a visit to Wembley came closer after Wigan were defeated 3-2 at home in the 2nd round.

The London Senior Cup trail continued with wins over Uxbridge and Edgware Town. A 17-year-old called Dave Beasant made his debut in the Town goal and a string of fine saves kept the score to 2-0. Between the Cup-ties Wimbledon were moving steadily up the table. By the end of February the Dons were in 2nd place.

	P	W	D	L	F	A	Pts
1 Bath City	26	11	11	4	32	21	33
2 WIMBLEDON	22	14	2	6	37	15	30
3 Grantham	26	11	7	8	44	29	29
4 Minehead	21	8	11	2	34	19	27
5 Kettering Town	21	9	9	3	31	21	27

Once again Cup success meant a fixture pile-up, with 25 matches to play in the final 12 weeks of the season. Before concentrating on chasing a third consecutive title the Dons had to face the bitter disappointment of an FA Trophy exit at the hands of Cheshire League Chorley. A 2-2 draw at Plough Lane, in which a young Steve Galliers starred for the visitors, was followed by another 2-2 draw in front of 6,000 fans in the replay. Chorley finally won the tie 2-0 at neutral Walsall in the second replay.

Driving home from Fellows Park with team skipper Dave Bassett, Noades hatched the plan that was to take the Dons into the Football League. He agreed a new bonus scheme to motivate the players to win the title again and decided to devote his energies to lobbying Football League Chairmen. In the end he visited all but four of those eligible to vote at the League AGM and received 38 promises of support — though not all of them materialised in the end.

After the Trophy exit, the Dons had 22 matches left to play and they only lost one as they stormed home to once again become Southern League Champions and holders of the London Senior Cup. The players had certainly earned their bonus.

The seven League games in March produced six wins and a draw, with the side returning to the top of the table following a crucial win at fellow title contenders Minehead. The mid-week trip to Devon was a tense affair with both teams having good chances before Jeff Bryant headed home a 77th minute corner to win both points.

At the end of March it was announced that only one club from the Southern League would be nominated for election — the side which finished highest in the table. Wimbledon, Yeovil, Kettering and Chelmsford all had good enough facilities but the Football League informed the Northern Premier League that none of their sides' grounds came up to the required standard.

Chairman Ron Noades informed the press of his determination to meet as many of his Football League counterparts as possible to press the Dons' case. He also unveiled plans to develop Plough Lane into a sporting complex, including an indoor sports hall seating 1,500. He rebutted any doubts about Wimbledon's financial position. 'We have greatly reduced our debts and now have an overdraft of only £17,000.'

On 5 April the Dons lost 1-0 at Dartford — their last defeat as a non-League club. They were unbeaten in their final thirteen games, including winning a replayed London Senior Cup-final with Staines at Dulwich. The crucial League match against Kettering Town drew over 4,000 to SW19. Managed by former Wolves player Derek Dougan, they were the only serious contenders for Wimbledon's title. The vital first goal for the Dons came in 42 minutes, when John Leslie headed home a corner; Jeff Bryant sewed things up in the last ten minutes. It was the first game Ron Noades had seen since the defeat at Chorley. He had spent every weekend on the motorway travelling to Football League grounds. Credit should go also to Jimmy Rose, Joe McElligott and Roger Easterly, who visited clubs on his behalf.

The race for the title continued until mid-April but, when Kettering crashed 5-1 at Yeovil, the Dons were confirmed as Champions for the third year running. They played what turned out to be their last Southern League match at Redditch and returned home victorious. The 3-0 win left Wimbledon five points clear at the top.

Strong lobbying by the Northern Premier League led to Altrincham joining Wimbledon as the non-League nominations for a League place. But the hard work of directors and players alike paid off on 17 June 1977. Workington's abysmal record of finishing bottom of Divison 4 three years in a row was a factor in making the Don's case unanswerable. When the counting stopped, Wimbledon had 27 votes and Workington only 21 — the Dons were in the League!

THREE SOUTHERN LEAGUE CHAMPIONSHIPS AT A GLANCE

SEASON 1974/1975

Date	Opponents	Comp.	Result
5 Aug.	**STAINES TOWN**	**F**	**3-1**
7 Aug.	WYCOMBE WANDERERS	F	2-1
10 Aug.	**CRYSTAL PALACE**	**F**	**1-0**
13 Aug.	**BISHOPS STORTFORD**	**F**	**1-3**
17 Aug.	NUNEATON BOROUGH	SL	0-2
20 Aug.	**YEOVIL TOWN**	**SL**	**1-0**
24 Aug.	**BARNET**	**SL**	**3-1**
27 Aug.	**BOGNOR REGIS TOWN**	**SLC**	**4-0**
31 Aug.	**TELFORD UNITED**	**SL**	**1-0**
4 Sept.	BOGNOR REGIS TOWN	SLC	3-1
7 Sept.	**BURTON ALBION**	**SL**	**3-2**
14 Sept.	BRACKNELL TOWN	FAC	3-1
18 Sept.	GUILDFORD & DORKING	SL	5-0
21 Sept.	YEOVIL TOWN	SL	1-0
24 Sept.	**GRANTHAM**	**SL**	**3-2**
28 Sept.	**CORINTHIAN CASUALS**	**LSC**	**1-0**
5 Oct.	**MAIDENHEAD UNITED**	**FAC**	**4-0**
8 Oct.	MAIDSTONE UNITED	SL	1-0
19 Oct.	**WOKINGHAM TOWN**	**FAC**	**2-0**
26 Oct.	**CHESHUNT**	**LSC**	**4-0**
2 Nov.	GUILDFORD & DORKING	FAC	3-0
4 Nov.	**ASHFORD TOWN**	**SLC**	**4-0**
9 Nov.	WEYMOUTH	SL	3-0
12 Nov.	**WEYMOUTH**	**SL**	**3-0**
16 Nov.	**TONBRIDGE**	**SL**	**4-1**
23 Nov.	**BATH CITY**	**FAC**	**1-0**
26 Nov.	**BIDEFORD TOWN**	**SLC**	**4-1**
3 Dec.	CAMBRIDGE CITY	SL	1-1
7 Dec.	**LEYTONSTONE**	**LSC**	**3-0**
14 Dec.	**KETTERING TOWN**	**FAC**	**2-0**
17 Dec.	**CAMBRIDGE CITY**	**SL**	**1-0**
21 Dec.	STOURBRIDGE	SL	1-2
26 Dec.	**DARTFORD**	**SL**	**1-1**
28 Dec.	ROMFORD	SL	2-0
1 Jan.	WEALDSTONE	SL	0-1
4 Jan.	BURNLEY	FAC	1-0
7 Jan.	**ATHERSTONE TOWN**	**SL**	**0-1**
11 Jan.	**SUTTON UNITED**	**FAT**	**3-1**
14 Jan.	**CHELMSFORD CITY**	**SL**	**2-0**
25 Jan.	LEEDS UNITED	FAC	0-0
1 Feb.	**KETTERING TOWN**	**FAT**	**1-0**
3 Feb.	**BARNET**	**LSC**	**1-1**
7 Feb.	KETTERING TOWN	SL	0-2
10 Feb.	**LEEDS UNITED**	**FAC**	**0-1**
15 Feb.	**KETTERING TOWN**	**SL**	**0-1**
17 Feb.	**STOURBRIDGE**	**SLC**	**3-1**
22 Feb.	**TELFORD UNITED**	**FAT**	**4-1**
25 Feb.	BARNET	LSC	2-1
1 Mar.	**NUNEATON BOROUGH**	**SL**	**1-0**
3 Mar.	CHELMSFORD CITY	SL	1-0
8 Mar.	SCARBOROUGH	FAT	0-1
10 Mar.	KETTERING TOWN	SLC	0-3
15 Mar.	**DAGENHAM**	**LSC**	**1-1**
18 Mar.	**DOVER**	**SL**	**0-0**
20 Mar.	DAGENHAM	LSC	2-1
22 Mar.	TONBRIDGE	SL	2-1
25 Mar.	**MAIDSTONE UNITED**	**SL**	**2-1**
29 Mar.	**MARGATE**	**SL**	**2-0**
31 Mar.	DARTFORD	SL	1-0
3 Apr.	**WEALDSTONE**	**SL**	**1-2**
5 Apr.	**BATH CITY**	**SL**	**0-1**
7 Apr.	GRANTHAM	SL	0-2
10 Apr.	BURTON ALBION	SL	0-0
12 Apr.	LEATHERHEAD	LSCT	2-0
14 Apr.	BATH CITY	SL	0-0
17 Apr.	**ROMFORD**	**SL**	**3-0**
19 Apr.	MARGATE	SL	3-3
21 Apr.	DOVER	SL	0-2
22 Apr.	**GUILDFORD & DORKING**	**SL**	**3-1**
24 Apr.	BARNET	SL	3-2
29 Apr.	**STOURBRIDGE**	**SL**	**2-0**
1 May.	**TELFORD UNITED**	**SL**	**1-1**
2 May	ATHERSTONE TOWN	SL	2-0

SEASON 1975/1976

Date	Opponents	Comp.	Result
2 Aug.	**WATFORD**	**F**	**2-4**
5 Aug.	**WYCOMBE WANDERERS**	**F**	**1-0**
9 Aug.	**EXETER CITY**	**F**	**2-0**
12 Aug.	**PORTSMOUTH**	**F**	**2-2**
16 Aug.	CAMBRIDGE CITY	SL	1-1
19 Aug.	**KETTERING TOWN**	**SLCC**	**1-0**
23 Aug.	**BURTON ALBION**	**SL**	**4-0**
26 Aug.	**HILLINGDON BOROUGH**	**SLC**	**3-0**
30 Aug.	HILLINGDON BOROUGH	SL	1-0
1 Sept.	HILLINGDON BOROUGH	SLC	2-0
6 Sept.	MARGATE	SL	2-1
9 Sept.	MAIDSTONE UNITED	SL	4-2
13 Sept.	GRANTHAM	SL	1-0
16 Sept.	**GRAVESEND & NORTHFLEET**	**SL**	**2-1**
20 Sept.	**KETTERING TOWN**	**SL**	**2-0**
24 Sept.	WIGAN ATHLETIC	SL/NPL Chall.	0-1
27 Sept.	**TELFORD UNITED**	**SL**	**3-0**
4 Sept.	ATHERSTONE TOWN	SL	1-2
11 Oct.	BEDFORD TOWN	SL	1-0
18 Oct.	**BATH CITY**	**SL**	**0-2**
21 Oct.	**ROMFORD**	**SLC**	**4-1**
25 Oct.	**FINCHLEY**	**LSC**	**2-1**
1 Nov.	**KINGSTONIAN**	**FAC**	**6-1**
8 Nov.	BURTON ALBION	SL	2-1
11 Nov.	**WIGAN ATHLETIC**	**SL/NPL Chall.**	**2-0 aet**
15 Nov.	**BEDFORD TOWN**	**SL**	**0-0**
22 Nov.	NUNEATON BOROUGH	FAC	1-0
25 Nov.	DUNSTABLE TOWN	SL	0-1
29 Nov.	TELFORD UNITED	SL	0-0
2 Dec.	**CHELMSFORD CITY**	**SLC**	**1-1**
6 Dec.	**ENFIELD**	**LSC**	**0-0**
13 Dec.	**BRENTFORD**	**FAC**	**0-2**
20 Dec.	**DOVER**	**SL**	**3-0**
23 Dec.	ENFIELD	LSC	0-1
26 Dec.	WEALDSTONE	SL	2-0
1 Jan.	KETTERING TOWN	SL	3-3
3 Jan.	NUNEATON BOROUGH	SL	0-1
10 Jan.	SUTTON UNITED	FAT	0-0
13 Jan.	**SUTTON UNITED**	**FAT**	**3-1**
17 Jan.	MARGATE	SL	0-2
19 Jan.	CHELMSFORD CITY	SLC	2-2
24 Jan.	**YEOVIL TOWN**	**SL**	**0-0**
26 Jan.	CHELMSFORD CITY	SLC	2-1
31 Jan.	**DAGENHAM**	**FAT**	**0-0**
2 Feb.	DAGENHAM	FAT	0-2
10 Feb.	**BURTON ALBION**	**SLC**	**2-0**
14 Feb.	**GRANTHAM**	**SL**	**2-1**
19 Feb.	**DOVER**	**SLC S/F**	**3-0**
21 Feb.	BATH CITY	SL	1-0
25 Feb.	YEOVIL TOWN	SL	2-1
28 Feb.	**TONBRIDGE**	**SL**	**3-0**
1 Mar.	**DOVER**	**SLC S/F**	**1-1**
3 Mar.	**CAMBRIDGE CITY**	**SL**	**0-0**
6 Mar.	CHELMSFORD CITY	SL	0-3
9 Mar.	**HILLINGDON BOROUGH**	**SL**	**2-2**
13 Mar.	**WEYMOUTH**	**SL**	**4-0**
16 Mar.	GRAVESEND & NORTHFLEET	SL	0-0
20 Mar.	**DUNSTABLE TOWN**	**SL**	**3-0**
24 Mar.	WEYMOUTH	SL	1-0
27 Mar.	STOURBRIDGE	SL	6-0
30 Mar.	**ATHERSTONE TOWN**	**SL**	**1-1**
3 Apr.	YEOVIL TOWN	SLC Final	1-1
6 Apr.	**CHELMSFORD CITY**	**SL**	**2-0**
10 Apr.	**YEOVIL TOWN**	**SLC Final**	**2-1**
13 Apr.	**STOURBRIDGE**	**SL**	**4-0**
17 Apr.	**MAIDSTONE UNITED**	**SL**	**1-1**
19 Apr.	DOVER	SL	2-1
22 Apr.	**NUNEATON BOROUGH**	**SL**	**2-0**
27 Apr.	**WEALDSTONE**	**SL**	**4-1**
30 Apr.	TONBRIDGE	SL	2-1
4 May	**BENEVENTO**	**AIC**	**4-0**
19 May	**SIRACUSA**	**AIC**	**3-0**
12 June	BENEVENTO	AIC	1-1
16 May	SIRACUSA	AIC	0-1
19 May	MONZA	AIC Final	0-1

SEASON 1976/1977

Date	*Opponents*	*Comp.*	*Result*
31 July	**READING**	**F**	**0-1**
3 Aug.	**COLCHESTER UNITED**	**F**	**1-2**
7 Aug.	SLOUGH TOWN	F	0-3
9 Aug.	**DERBY COUNTY XI**	**F**	**3-0**
11 Aug.	WYCOMBE WANDERERS	F	1-2
14 Aug.	DULWICH HAMLET	F	4-1
17 Aug.	**LEYTONSTONE**	**F**	**3-2**
21 Aug.	ROMFORD	SLC	0-2
24 Aug.	**ROMFORD**	**SLC**	**2-0**
28 Aug.	**A.P.LEAMINGTON**	**SL**	**0-0**
31 Aug.	GRAVESEND & NORTHFLEET	SL	0-1
4 Sept.	KETTERING TOWN	SL	0-1
11 Sept.	**WEALDSTONE**	**SL**	**5-1**
14 Sept.	**ARSENAL XI**	**F**	**5-0**
18 Sept.	**CHELMSFORD CITY**	**SL**	**2-1**
21 Sept.	ROMFORD	SLC	2-0 aet
25 Sept.	**BURTON ALBION**	**SL**	**2-0**
2 Oct.	WEYMOUTH	SL	2-1
5 Oct.	**YEOVIL TOWN**	**SLCC**	**1-2 aet**
11 Oct.	**ATHERSTONE TOWN**	**SL**	**3-1**
12 Oct.	WALTHAMSTOW AVENUE	LSC	1-1
16 Oct.	MAIDSTONE UNITED	SL	0-2
19 Oct.	**WALTHAMSTOW AVENUE**	**LSC**	**1-0**
23 Oct.	**BATH CITY**	**SL**	**0-2**
26 Oct.	BARNET	SLC	1-1
2 Nov.	**BARNET**	**SLC**	**2-3**
6 Nov.	**MARGATE**	**SL**	**2-1**
9 Nov.	**RUNCORN**	**SL/NPL Chall.**	**0-1**
13 Nov.	BATH CITY	SL	0-1
20 Nov.	**WOKING**	**FAC**	**1-0**
27 Nov.	YEOVIL TOWN	SL	1-1
30 Nov.	RUNCORN	SL/NPL Chall.	3-1
4 Dec.	BARKING	LSC	1-0
14 Dec.	LEATHERHEAD	FAC	3-1
21 Dec.	**DARTFORD**	**SL**	**1-0**
27 Dec.	HILLINGDON BOROUGH	SL	2-0
1 Jan.	**BEDFORD TOWN**	**SL**	**3-0**
8 Jan.	**MIDDLESBROUGH**	**FAC**	**0-0**
11 Jan.	MIDDLESBROUGH	FAC	0-1
19 Jan.	GRANTHAM	FAT	1-0
22 Jan.	**UXBRIDGE**	**LSC**	**2-0**
24 Jan.	NUNEATON BOROUGH	SL	0-1
29 Jan.	**GRAVESEND & NORTHFLEET**	**SL**	**2-1**
5 Feb.	**WIGAN ATHLETIC**	**FAT**	**3-2**
8 Feb.	**REDDITCH UNITED**	**SL**	**3-0**
12 Feb.	**NUNEATON BOROUGH**	**SL**	**4-0**
15 Feb.	ATHERSTONE TOWN	SL	2-0
19 Feb.	**EDGWARE TOWN**	**LSC**	**2-0**
22 Feb.	A.P.LEAMINGTON	SL	3-0
26 Feb.	**CHORLEY**	**FAT**	**2-2**
1 Mar.	CHORLEY	FAT	2-2 aet
5 Mar.	BURTON ALBION	SL	1-0
7 Mar.	CHORLEY	FAT	0-2
9 Mar.	DOVER	SL	1-1
12 Mar.	**WEYMOUTH**	**SL**	**1-0**
14 Mar.	**DOVER**	**SL**	**2-1**
19 Mar.	**HITCHIN TOWN**	**LSC**	**3-0**
22 Mar.	MINEHEAD	SL	1-0
26 Mar.	**MAIDSTONE UNITED**	**SL**	**2-1**
29 Mar.	**GRANTHAM**	**SL**	**1-0**
1 Apr.	MARGATE	SL	3-0
5 Apr.	DARTFORD	SL	0-1
9 Apr.	BEDFORD TOWN	SL	2-0
11 Apr.	**HILLINGDON BOROUGH**	**SL**	**1-1**
16 Apr.	CHELMSFORD CITY	SL	2-1
18 Apr.	**TELFORD UNITED**	**SL**	**0-0**
23 Apr.	STAINES TOWN	LSC Final	0-0 aet
25 Apr.	**KETTERING TOWN**	**SL**	**2-0**
29 Apr.	GRANTHAM	SL	0-0
2 May	TELFORD UNITED	SL	3-1
4 May	**MINEHEAD**	**SL**	**1-0**
7 May	**YEOVIL TOWN**	**SL**	**1-0**
12 May	WEALDSTONE	SL	0-0
14 May	REDDITCH UNITED	SL	3-0
17 May	STAINES TOWN	LSC F Replay	1-0

1974/1975 LEAGUE TABLE

	P	W	D	L	F	A	Pts
Wimbledon	**42**	**25**	**7**	**10**	**63**	**33**	**57**
Nuneaton Borough	42	23	8	11	56	37	54
Yeovil Town	42	21	9	12	64	34	51
Kettering Town	42	20	10	12	73	41	50
Burton Albion	42	18	13	11	54	48	49
Bath City	42	20	8	14	63	50	48
Margate	42	17	12	13	64	64	47
Wealdstone	42	17	11	14	62	61	45
Telford United	42	16	13	13	55	56	45
Chelmsford City	42	16	12	14	62	51	44
Grantham	42	16	11	15	70	62	43
Dover	42	15	13	14	43	53	43
Maidstone United	42	15	12	15	52	50	42
Atherstone Town	42	14	14	14	48	53	42
Weymouth	42	13	13	16	66	58	38
Stourbridge	42	13	12	17	56	70	38
Cambridge City	42	11	14	17	51	56	36
Tonbridge	42	11	12	19	44	66	34
Romford	42	10	13	19	46	62	33
Dartford	42	9	13	20	52	70	31
Barnet	42	10	9	23	44	76	29
Guildford/Dorking Utd.	42	10	5	27	45	82	25

1975/1976 LEAGUE TABLE

	P	W	D	L	F	A	Pts
Wimbledon	**42**	**26**	**10**	**6**	**74**	**29**	**62**
Yeovil Town	42	21	12	9	68	35	54
Atherstone Town	42	18	15	9	56	55	51
Maidstone United	42	17	16	9	52	39	50
Nuneaton Borough	42	16	18	8	41	33	50
Gravesend/N'fleet	42	16	18	8	49	47	50
Grantham	42	15	14	13	56	47	44
Dunstable	42	17	9	16	52	43	43
Bedford Town	42	13	17	12	55	51	43
Burton Albion	42	17	9	16	52	53	43
Margate	42	15	12	15	62	60	42
Hillingdon Borough	42	13	14	15	61	54	40
Telford United	42	14	12	16	54	51	40
Chelmsford City	42	13	14	15	52	57	40
Kettering Town	42	11	17	14	48	52	39
Bath City	42	11	16	15	62	57	38
Weymouth	42	13	9	20	51	67	35
Dover	42	8	18	16	51	50	34
Wealdstone	42	12	9	21	61	82	33
Tonbridge A.F.C.	42	11	11	20	45	70	33
Cambridge City	42	8	15	19	41	67	31
Stourbridge	42	10	9	23	38	72	29

1976/1977 LEAGUE TABLE

	P	W	D	L	F	A	Pts
Wimbledon	**42**	**28**	**7**	**7**	**64**	**22**	**63**
Minehead	42	23	12	7	73	39	58
Kettering Town	42	20	16	6	66	46	56
Bath City	42	20	15	7	51	30	55
Nuneaton Borough	42	20	11	11	52	35	51
Bedford Town	42	17	14	11	54	47	48
Yeovil Town	42	15	16	11	54	42	46
Dover	42	13	16	13	46	43	42
Grantham	42	14	12	16	55	50	40
Maidstone United	42	13	14	15	46	50	40
Gravesend/N'fleet	42	13	13	16	38	43	39
AP.Leamington	42	12	15	15	44	53	39
Redditch	42	12	14	16	45	54	38
Wealdstone	42	13	12	17	54	66	38
Hillingdon Borough	42	14	10	18	45	59	38
Atherstone Town	42	14	9	19	41	49	37
Weymouth	42	16	5	21	53	73	37
Dartford	42	13	10	19	52	57	36
Telford United	42	11	12	19	36	50	34
Chelmsford City	42	9	13	20	56	68	31
Burton Albion	42	10	10	22	41	52	30
Margate	42	9	10	23	47	85	28

ABOVE: Dejection among the Gillingham players, including a young Gary Armstrong (with the ball) after Wimbledon's third goal in the Football League Cup-tie. BELOW: Halifax's Gennoe and Bradley lie flat out as the Dons' Billy Holmes look worried.

From Innocence to Experience 1977-1978

Excitement turns to reality

If ever the old managerial cliché 'It's a game of two halves' could be applied to a season, it was this one. Football League new boys Wimbledon struggled for months to make an impression, hovering dangerously close to the re-election zone. Then, from February onwards, following Dario Gradi's appointment as manager, they climbed steadily to mid-table respectability.

There was a real sense of optimism as Wimbledon began training in July 1977. 'I would not go as far as to say we will win promotion at this stage because I don't know what the competition is going to be like,' Chairman Ron Noades commented. 'But fans have got used to success and I don't see why it should not stay that way.' Manager Allen Batsford was more cautious: 'It's going to take a lot of hard work,' he said. 'I shall be happy to consolidate with a mid-table position in our first season.'

Despite their elevation the Club decided to remain part-time. Dickie Guy, stalwart goalkeeper for nearly a decade explained — 'How can I afford to go full-time at my age? I do quite well at the moment thanks to my football money plus my job as a tally clerk in the West India docks. Most of the lads have good jobs and don't want to give them up'.

Wimbledon's decision was hailed at the time as an historic one which, if successful, would pave the way for other clubs to copy. Reality was different and within six months Wimbledon had become full-time following a run of disappointing results.

Throughout July Batsford was searching for players to add to his squad. Most of the players who had served the Dons during their victorious Southern League campaigns were retained. Among the exceptions were long-serving skipper Ian Cooke, whose commitments at his bank prevented him giving the time needed for League football. Eventually five new players were signed — goalkeeper Richard Teale, defender David Galvin, mid-fielders Steve Galliers and Willie Smith and forward Paul Denny.

Pre-season preparations went well, with four friendlies arranged to mould the side together. Third Division Colchester won 3-1 at Plough Lane before victories over Hereford, 4-1 at home and Gravesend, 1-0 away. First Division QPR were the final opponents in a testimonial for Dave Clement. Fielding their full first team they won 3-1 in SW19 during the week before the season began.

The Priestfield Stadium in Gillingham was the venue for the Dons' first competitive game as a League club. The Kent side, then in the Third Division, provided a tough test in a League Cup 1st Round, 1st leg tie. After deservedly trailing at half-time, Wimbledon fought back and a Billy Holmes header secured a 1-1 draw. The 2nd leg, at Plough Lane on the following Tuesday, saw the Dons in fine form and goals from Dave Bassett, Roger Connell and that man Holmes again saw them through to Round Two.

History was made on 20 August 1977 as Wimbledon made their debut in Division Four. Although the opponents — Halifax Town — lacked glamour, a crowd of 4,616 was disappointing. Chairman Ron Noades had expected a 'gate' of 10,000 and his prediction of an average crowd of 5,500 was clearly going to be wide of the mark.

If things were disappointing off pitch, on the field, manager Batsford was furious after his team was held to a 3-3 draw. Jeff Bryant scored the Club's first League goal and, despite leading 3-2 with less than five minutes to go, the Dons could not hang on for a famous victory.

The reality of life in this League was hammered home on the following Monday evening, when over 11,000 saw the Dons easily beaten at Brentford's Griffin Park. The 4-1 reverse led to Batsford taking swift action by axing the Club's best known player — goalkeeper Dickie Guy — and replacing him with Richard Teale. The result was a much-improved performance at Torquay, where a late Roger Connell goal salvaged a point.

The Dons bowed out of the League Cup at the second hurdle — beaten 4-0 by Spurs at White Hart Lane. More disappointment followed as Wimbledon were held by Southport at home. The 2-2 draw had Batsford complaining: 'This was another poor performance, especially in defence. We simply chucked away a point today'.

The pressures of League football were forgotten on 6 September as Wimbledon honoured Ian Cooke. A testimonial match with Crystal Palace attracted 2,422 to Plough Lane and Cooke himself scored the first goal in a 2-1 win. Since joining the Club in 1962 he had appeared in over 600 games and scored more than 300 goals. His move to Slough Town in August had severed the last link with the Club's amateur days.

Back on the Fourth Division trail the need for a rapid improvement was rammed home by three successive defeats. The long journey to Hartlepool proved fruitless as the Dons were defeated 2-0. A mid-week local derby with Aldershot produced an improved performance, but an 89th minute penalty save ensured the visitors returned to Hampshire with the points. At Scunthorpe the side was outplayed and lost 3-0; already lacking confidence they suffered a further blow when defender Dave Donaldson was injured early in the second half.

After seven games Wimbledon had three points and were second to bottom of the table. Only Rochdale were below them and they had a game in hand. Chairman Ron Noades was not unduly perturbed, though he observed 'It's really a question of players' attitudes. Some may not relish the hardness of Fourth Division football'.

ABOVE: Billy Edwards scores the lone Wimbledon goal against Aldershot at Plough Lane. BELOW: Geoff Davies celebrates while Southport goalkeeper Harrison looks in vain to the referee for help. In fact Billy Edwards had just scored the second Wimbledon goal.

ABOVE: Geoff Davies scores the second goal at home to Newport County. BELOW: Billy Holmes rounds off the 3-0 win against Newport with his lobbed third goal.

Batsford resigns as Dons slump

With little money available, manager Allen Batsford was forced to look for free transfers. Experienced pro Phil Summerill was signed from Millwall for nothing and joined a side which was assuming a familiar look: Teale in goal with Kevin Tilley and Billy Edwards at full back. Jeff Bryant was partnered by Dave Donaldson or Dave Galvin at centre back just behind a midfield of Dave Bassett, Steve Galliers and Geoff Davies. Summerill was immediately drafted in to join Billy Holmes and John Leslie up front.

The effect of the change was immediate as, at the eighth attempt, the Dons recorded their first win — a 2-0 triumph over Northampton Town at Plough Lane. It was Summerill himself who volleyed home the vital second goal in the 38th minute.

Visibly growing in confidence, Wimbledon comfortably beat Newport County at home the following Tuesday. The 3-0 success saw a first goal for the Club from Dave Galvin and others from Geoff Davies and Billy Holmes. Visiting manager Ron Addison commented: 'We were thoroughly, comprehensively, systematically taken apart. If Wimbledon play like that they will win the division'.

Any notions that these wins were the start of a sustained push up the table were extinguished by a run of six matches which produced only one win. At Elm Park, Reading, the Dons were lucky to come away with a 2-2 draw as a young student named Lawrie Sanchez made his debut for the Royals. Grimsby Town were less generous and recorded a 3-1 win as Summerill scored his third goal in four games.

After a 0-0 draw in driving rain against Crewe Alexandra, the Dons recorded their first away win of their short League career — at Bournemouth by two goals to one. Hard-to-please manager Allen Batsford moaned that the Dons should have won more comfortably: 'We would have done if our finishing had been sharper,' he said. 'But it's great to win away at last. It should help us to relax and believe in ourselves.'

The missed chances were certainly a concern but more worrying was the defence. After two 3-1 defeats at home to Southend and away to Darlington — twenty-nine goals had been conceded in fifteen matches. But Dario Gradi, newly installed as assistant manager, sounded optimistic. 'Wimbledon are learning to adjust to the pace and standards of the Fourth Division. I think we will consolidate our position this season.'

Gradi was appointed in a full-time capacity and boss Batsford joined him, acknowledging the demands of the job. 'There is an awful lot of work to do at the Club, negotiations for two or three players we require, checking other teams and so on, I need to spend more time here.'

He continued: 'The players are giving up evening training and coming in every afternoon instead. We are as fit as anyone, but need to work at ball control technique and match situations'. He sounded a cheeful and optimistic note, 'We are weathering the storm. Coming from the Southern League, I'm finding it just as expected and I'm only disappointed with one or two aspects of our play. When people said we'd get promotion at the first attempt, I warned it was not being realistic. Our aim is to consolidate and, if we can get halfway, I'll be most happy'. Wise but realistic words from a man whose team was still in the re-election zone — fourth from bottom.

Late October saw the Dons paying its dues to its Southern League past. As reigning champions, Wimbledon were host to Dartford, the Cup winners, in a challenge match.

Goals from recalled Connell plus efforts from Davies and Galliers ensured a 3-2 win.

League form improved too with a run of five games without defeat. However, four of the matches were at home and only one win, the 2-1 defeat of York City, was recorded. By this time Dickie Guy had regained his number one shirt and Jeff Bryant had replaced Kevin Tilley at right back. Up front Billy Holmes had left for Hereford United, meaning Paul Denny came into the side on a permanent basis.

However, perhaps the lowest point of the season was reached during this run with a first round FA Cup exit at the hands of Isthmian League Enfield. A side whom Wimbledon would have expected to beat in previous seasons ultimately won fairly easily. The Dons team seemed to lack belief in themselves and Batsford summed it up by saying: 'Winning used to be a habit with us and now we've lost it. We must start to cultivate that habit now'.

As if to emphasise their lack of form Wimbledon lost their grip on a trophy which they had won in the two previous seasons. The annual match between the Southern and Northern Premier League Champions took place, over two legs, in early December. In those pre-Conference days the winners could call themselves the top non-League side but the Dons' election to the Football League changed this in 1977.

A Paul Denny goal ensured a 1-1 draw at Plough Lane against a determined Boston United side, who followed this up with a 1-0 win at York Street a week later. Jim Kabia's goal, on the stroke of half-time, saw the trophy heading north to Lincolnshire. Whether these games served to do anything more than help deflate an already leg-weary side is open to question.

The Dons approached the Christmas period out of the Cups and in nineteenth place in the League table. A disastrous run saw the team slide once again into the bottom four and led to the departure of Allen Batsford. In the sixteen days from 17 December the team played five matches, four ended in defeat, and three goals were conceded in each one.

They began at Huddersfield in a re-arranged fixture and returned south on the wrong end of a 3-0 score line. Having inherited Workington's fixture list, the Dons returned north to bottom of the table Rochdale on Boxing Day. Another 3-0 defeat, against a poor side, illustrated how vital self-belief had drained from the side.

A 3-3 home draw with Doncaster Rovers two days later was marked by the home debut of a talented young left-winger called Steve Parsons. He immediately impressed with his play, particularly with his left foot and the accuracy of his free kicks and corners. The last day of 1977 saw top-of-the-table Watford win 3-1 at Plough Lane. The 7,234 crowd was destined to be the highest home attendance of the season.

Yet another 3-0 away defeat followed at Swansea City, after an incident which had elements of farce. Centre back Dave Galvin was left behind at a hotel in Bristol after the team had stopped for a pre-match meal. A sheepish Batsford admitted it was his fault. 'Somewhere along the line my maths went wrong.'

The eleven players whom the Dons put out at the Vetch Field were outplayed by the high-flying Swans. It was too much for Batsford, who resigned during the week following the game. He was obviously unhappy as he told the press: 'I felt I was gradually being squeezed out. Decisions were being taken over my head, decisions that were my responsibility. They went and signed a two-year contract on totally inadequate training facilities, for instance. The part-time set up should have been changed more quickly . . . I never knew whether money was available for new players, or not'. Batsford also felt that Ron Noades had interfered with the playing side of the

Club; in particular he did not like the lack of consultation over Dario Gradi's appointment to run the revamped youth scheme.

Noades responded: 'My view on this is that Dario was one of the best people to run our youth scheme, which is very important to the long term future of the Club'. He also blamed the team's form for Batsford's departure, commenting: 'I think the effects of all those defeats in a row got on top of him — the run of bad results got too much for him'.

The players were shocked when they heard the announcement. 'We were just stunned when we heard Allen had resigned', said skipper Dave Bassett. 'It didn't sink in at first. After all, I'd been with him eight years, Dave Donaldson had been with him nine, Roger Connell seven and Billy Edwards eight. Allen has always been totally sincere, completely honest. You always knew where you stood with him. He pulled no punches and he was always a winner.'

His 37-year-old successor Dario Gradi had spent his playing career with Tooting and Mitcham and Sutton United before joining the Football Association as a coach. After six years in charge of the youth team at Chelsea he had a short spell in the manager's chair at Sutton. An offer to join Derby County as assistant to Colin Murphy was too good to refuse but, after only eight months, he had to quit following the arrival of Tommy Docherty.

It was then that Noades had stepped in to bring him to Wimbledon to run the youth set-up. His contacts in the game and his emphasis on youth caused a rapid change at Plough Lane. He was determined to make the players go full-time and transform results. In both of these he was immediately successful — the Club was fully full-time by the end of the season and, after struggling to four wins in 25 games under Batsford, another 10 wins were recorded in the final 21 fixtures.

Roger Connell steadies himself and then fires over from a yard late in the 0-0 draw with Barnsley. Future Republic of Ireland manager Mick McCarthy looks on.

ABOVE: Kevin Tilley rides a sliding tackle from Southend's Frank Banks in the 3-1 home defeat. BELOW: Steve Parsons is beaten to the ball by Alan Garner of Watford on the last day of 1977.

Gradi transforms the Club

Dario Gradi was determined to change the playing side of the Club. 'I want a miracle,' he announced boldly. 'I don't want to just get this team out of the bottom four. I want to get them right out of the Fourth Division.' He also pledged to make the players full-time as soon as possible, saying 'The Club has always wanted to go full-time eventually. It means the players are working at it all the time and we should be more successful'. His emphasis was clearly going to be on youth as he promised to introduce some younger players.

He was as good as his word, taking eighteen months to achieve promotion but altering the team straight away. Geoff Davies, who played almost every match under Batsford, did not play for Gradi. Dickie Guy, Kevin Tilley and Billy Edwards were all axed within a month, while Dave Bassett played only ten more games before becoming assistant manager.

A good illustration of the pace of change under Gradi came from the programme at Southport. Bad weather caused the postponement of the original fixture in January and, when the programme was re-issued in April, the Dons' team showed eight changes from the published side.

Gradi's first month in charge saw four matches survive the weather and a creditable win and two draws were obtained as he shuffled his team around. His first match as manager saw the Dons come from behind to force a draw in the 'derby' with high-flying Brentford.

Despite going behind after 11 minutes, Wimbledon fought back to record their second away win at Halifax. Second half goals from Jeff Bryant and Paul Denny ensured the win. But a disappointing home defeat by Torquay followed despite intense second half pressure. Although his side was in the bottom four, Dickie Guy remained optimisic. 'All the players feel we can finish at least half way up the table,' he said. 'We've only got to string a few results together to see us clear.'

In fact, Guy was to be one of the first victims of the Gradi purge. The signs were ominous as goalkeeper Ray Goddard was signed from Millwall for £4,000. Also signed the same week were three young players who had all worked with Gradi at Derby — Alan Cork, Steve Ketteridge and Fran Cowley.

With Dickie Guy reporting late, after dealing with frozen pipes at his Bromley home, Goddard made his debut against Scunthorpe United. The match turned out to be the end for Guy — a Wimbledon institution — but the beginning for a young man destined to have a big future at the Club. Eighteen-year-old Alan Cork impressed the crowd of only 1,603 with a strong running display. But there was little to cheer on a freezing afternoon as the match eneded goalless.

Gradi's new-look side was already taking shape. Cork was joined up front by Roger Connell who replaced out-of-favour Phil Summerill. Two wingers supported the front men, John Leslie and young Steve Parsons, fresh from non-League Walton. A midfield of Dave Bassett and Paul Denny were employed in front of a four man defence consisting of Jeff Bryant, Dave Donaldson, Dave Galvin and Terry Eames. Between the posts Goddard immediately stemmed the flow of goals. Having leaked 49 goals prior to his appointment, Gradi's side conceded only 15 more that season.

With a secure defence the team began to play with increasing confidence and results began to improve. A freezing Monday evening in February attracted only 1,440 people

to Plough Lane — the lowest gate of the season — but they left happy with a 3-0 wi
over Hartlepool. Dave Galvin scored twice but it was Roger Connell who wa
dominating the attack. Having scored the opener against Hartlepool, he followed u
with the equaliser in the drawn match with Reading. This game was an experimen
with Friday night football, which was not repeated after only 2,567 turned up — man
from Berkshire.

A first half pair from Connell set up a 3-0 away win at Northampton, whic
completed 'the double' over a poor Cobblers' side. Then, with the transfer deadlin
approaching, Gradi made two further signings: Les Briley from £16,000 fro
Hereford and Dave Bradley 'on loan' from Manchester United for the rest of th
season. To help pay for Briley the Club sold its 16-seater team 'bus and then bought i
back on hire purchase!

With the team now out of the four re-election places, there was an air of optimis
about the Club. It was announced that Dave Bassett was to become full-time assistan
manager, taking responsibility for the Reserves and helping with the coaching. 'Harr
hasn't got to prove himself,' said Grad; 'He knows the players well, has marvellou
non-League contacts and is a good businessman. He will take some of the weight of
my mind'. Bassett himself said: 'I'm delighted and I hope I can go into full-tim
management from now on'.

Les Briley made his debut on the 0-0 draw at Crewe. He replaced John Leslie wit
eight minutes to go, in a match which demonstrated how difficult the Dons ha
become to beat. Wimbledon's unbeaten run came to an end at the Recreation Groun
in Aldershot as the promotion-chasing home side won 3-1.

Manager Gradi was not despondent, believing that his side was now achieving wha
he had hoped for when he was appointed. 'What pleases me' he said, 'is that we are o
course for what we want — safety from re-election and a professinal club'. In a tigh
division, the Dons had climbed to 18th place, only seven points behind Swansea in 5t
spot.

Steve Parsons lets fly but this effort flew wide at home to Torquay United.

ABOVE: Panic stations in the Scunthorpe defence but none of the Dons, from left Dave Galvin, Alan Cork, Paul Denny and John Leslie, can get a decisive touch. CENTRE: Roger Connell climbs highest as Hartlepool are beaten 3-0 in front of only 1,440 fans — the lowest crowd to see a League game at Plough Lane. BELOW: Phil Summerill and Les Briley race for the ball during the 3-1 defeat at Aldershot.

ABOVE: Roger Connell has this point blank shot saved by the Bournemouth 'keeper Baker at Plough Lane in March 1978. BELOW: John Leslie shoots for goal at home to Huddersfield.

A stylish finish

The final six weeks of the season saw Wimbledon playing with confidence and style. It was hard to see how they had struggled at the wrong end of the table for so long, as in twelve games they ran in twenty-five goals with only twelve in reply.

The visit of AFC Bournemouth was a day of firsts. There were home debuts for Les Briley and Dave Bradley — in for Bassett and Eames — and Alan Cork scored his first goal for the Club. It was a close-range shot, following a Connell flick on from a perfect Parsons corner. 'We played some fine football,' said Gradi after the 3-1 win. 'Everybody did well and I certainly did not expect the team to come good this early.'

Despite losing at Roots Hall, to a Southend side poised to achieve Third Division football, Wimbledon's squad emerged with credit from a 1-0 defeat. Indeed, Southend boss Dave Smith tipped the Dons for promotion the following season. 'I think Dario has done a great job in such a short time,' said Smith, 'And because of the work he has done, I think Wimbledon must be a good bet for promotion next time. I was impressed with their style of play. They showed good teamwork, worked hard and played to their strengths. I must admit we were lucky to win.'

The Dons grabbed four points over Easter with two comfortable wins over Doncaster and Rochdale. Firstly, Jeff Bryant and Alan Cork were on target in a 2-0 win at Belle Vue, a match in which the defence emerged with great credit after withstanding fierce first half pressure. Then on Easter Monday, bottom-of-the-table Rochdale provided little resistance, as Wimbledon won 5-1 to record the biggest League win so far.

Gradi was buoyant. 'Our recent matches have seen us vastly improved,' he said. 'It's been an accumulation of things really, barring Aldershot and Southend the results have gone right for us. We were very organised against Doncaster and Rochdale. Whenever one of their players got the ball the right person came to shut him down.'

On All Fools Day the Dons made the short journey to Watford and were on the wrong end of a 2-0 scoreline. The Graham Taylor/Elton John partnership that was to carry the Hornets into Division One in four seasons was reaching the end of its first year. A crowd of 11,212 — the biggest to see Wimbledon in League action that year — packed Vicarage Road to see their favourites maintain their huge lead at the top of the table.

Three days later Wimbledon threw away a two goal lead as Grimsby held them to a 2-2 draw, but Gradi rated the display the best since he took over. Then John Leslie and Jeff Bryant scored as the Dons gained revenge for an early season defeat at Huddersfield. That 2-0 win was another excellent performance by a young side gaining confidence by the match.

On Tuesday 11 April 1978, nearly 5,000 people turned up at Plough Lane to pay tribute to Dickie Guy. The Club's most famous player starred in a 3-0 testimonial win over First Division Chelsea. His penalty save from Leeds' Peter Lorimer in the FA Cup in January 1975 had made him a household name. But for Dons' fans it was his consistency over nearly a decade that made him so popular. Between 17 January 1970 and 27 August 1977, he missed only one match out of 449. In all he played nearly 600 matches for Wimbledon and in the last three Southern League seasons conceded only 34 goals in 126 matches.

Back on the points trail only a disputed late penalty denied the Dons victory at York City. Connell was on target for the visitors and two days later 'Big Rog' led the way again with two in a remarkable 5-0 win at Southport. It proved to be the only visit Wimbledon was to make to Haig Avenue as the Sandgrounders were voted out of the League at the end of the season, replaced by Wigan Athletic.

Two more wins followed — 2-0 at home to Stockport and 1-0 away to Newport — before a 3-2 defeat in the final game at Barnsley's Oakwell ground. Roger Connell's two goals in that game took him to fourteen, making him the top scorer for the fourth successive year. The Dons finished thirteenth — a position they would probably have settled for nine months earlier.

Gradi was quietly pleased with how his first six month in charge had gone. 'I think the reason for survival has been the way the Club has come together. The players have done what I asked and disciplined themselves well both on and off the field. In particular, the directors have been a great help. The money they gave me for Les Briley had made all the difference. It was a bold decision for them to make with such an inexperienced manager. Of course winning has helped but our luck with injuries has been another factor.'

Roger Connell was positive about the contribution of the young manager. 'No disrespect to Allen, but Dario is far more professional. He gives the older players more leeway but expects us to set an example. Full-time training has made us fitter and more alert. We all think the last quarter of the season has shown our potential and the prospects for next season must be good.' He concluded his thoughts for next term by adding 'Promotion is all down to character — and I think we have that character'.

Ron Noades was also upbeat about the financial prospects of the Club: 'What we've done this season is to accomplish enough to show a weekly profit despite increasing outgoings, such as wages. Diversification is the only way to survive in this business and we are now running several companies under the main company. Once the night club starts to function full time, then the success will be obvious'.

Asked to comment on the gates he repied: 'Considering we have spent most of the season in the bottom four, the crowds have been what I expected. The potential is there if we start next season as we ended this one'. Everyone at the Club was looking forward to the 1978-79 season with eager anticipation.

ABOVE: Roger Connell loses out to Watford's Ian Booth in front of 11,212 fans at Vicarage Road. BELOW: The only goal at Newport. Jeff Bryant is about to celebrate a goal from Roger Connell (out of picture).

ABOVE: Jeff Bryant (arm raised) is obscured by John Leslie as he salutes the first Wimbledon goal in the Football League. LEFT: Geoff Davies, on his debut, wins this midfield duel against Halifax. RIGHT: Geoff Davies, in determined mood, late on at Enfield.

Memorable Matches 1977-8

20 August 1977: FOOTBALL LEAGUE DIVISION FOUR
Wimbledon 3 *Bryant, Davies, Connell*
Halifax Town 3 *Carroll 2, Bell*

Sloppy defending and a touch of big occasion nerves cost Wimbledon victory on their Football League debut. Leading 3-2 with only minutes on the clock the Dons lost concentration and allowed Derek Bell to salvage a point for a poor Halifax side.

The Dons' team had three changes from the side that dumped 3rd Division Gillingham out of the League Cup in midweek. In came Geoff Davies, Glen Aitken and Dave Galvin for Kevin Tilley, Billy Edwards and Dave Bassett. Nine Dons men were playing their first match in the Football League, while skipper for the day Dave Donaldson became, at 35, the oldest man to make his League debut. Dave Galvin, with years of experience at Gillingham, was making his first appearance in a Wimbledon shirt.

Everything went well for the home supporters in the 4,616 crowd at first. They pressed hard for an early goal but then fell behind after 40 minutes to one of sheer stupidity. Goalkeeper Dickie Guy threw the ball out to Dave Donaldson who failed to notice the lurking Joe Carroll. The Halifax man dispossessed Donaldson and coolly slotted past Guy.

Wimbledon battled back hard and six minutes after the restart Jeff Bryant scored the historic first League goal when he stabbed the ball home following a free kick. However, Halifax regained the lead soon aferwards when Dons' defence again failed to react, and the ever dangerous Carroll latched on to a through ball to score his second.

New signing Geoff Davies, who had a fine match, laid on a 70th minute equaliser for John Leslie with an intelligent crossfield run and accurate pass. Then it was all down to the last hectic five minutes as Roger Connell gave Dons the scent of victory with a 20 yard rocket, a quite astonishing goal in contrast with his subdued display.

But Halifax were not to be denied, Derek Bell floating home a late equaliser following a corner with the home defence stranded. Three players were booked: Aitken of Wimbledon and Carroll and Bradley of Halifax, but it was never a dirty match.

Alan Ball Senior, the Halifax manager, had some harsh words for the Dons afterwards. 'They won't set the Fourth Division alight unless they buy some more players, but they will certainly give a lot of teams a hard game. They are strong and hand out a lot of stick for a southern side. But I can only see them consolidating this season.'

Dons' boss Allen Batsford was even more critical: 'It was a disgraceful performance all round. We played without enthusiasm and were nowhere near aggressive enough. The trouble is some of my players think all they have to do is go out there'.

However, goalkeeper Dickie Guy had no doubts that Wimbledon would do well in Division 4. 'We must be one of the strongest sides to be elected to the Football League,' he said. 'I shall be sick if we don't go up. It might take us a few matches to settle down but I'm sure we'll be there at the finish.'

The match generated intense media coverage, with a report on the evening BBC news bulletin. 10,000 programmes were sent out to eight different countries as well as to all corners of the British Isles.

WIMBLEDON: Guy, Bryant, Galvin, Donaldson, Aitken, Davies, Galliers, Smith, Connell, Holmes, Leslie. Sub: Eames (Not Used).
HALIFAX: Gennoe, Flavell, Loska, Smith, Dunleary, Bradley, Carroll, Johnson, Bullock, Bell, Horsfall.
CROWD: 4,616 REFEREE: D. Smith (Essex)

24 September 1977: FOOTBALL LEAGUE DIVISION FOUR
Wimbledon 2 *Holmes, Summerill*
Northampton Town 0

A win at last! At the eighth attempt, struggling Wimbledon finally broke their Football League duck with a win over Northampton Town. Two first half goals in three minutes sunk the visitors and made history for the Dons.

Billy Holmes put Wimbledon ahead with a 35th minute header. Kevin Tilley, a late replacement for the injured Dave Donaldson, opened the stubborn defence with an accurate cross and Holmes had no difficulty in nodding home a simple chance.

Then Phil Summerill, making his Dons debut after a free transfer move from Millwall four days earlier, made his mark by hitting the clincher with a spectacular volley from 12 yards. Wimbledon had other chances from Geoff Davies and Steve Galliers in the first half and all Northampton offered in return was a wild effort from Don Martin.

After the break they looked dangerous in a couple of raids and 'keeper Richard Teale had to make a stupendous save from George Riley. In truth the second period belonged to Wimbledon, but they could not turn their superiority into goals. Jeff Bryant headed onto the post, 'keeper Stuart Garnham could only fend out a Holmes free kick and Summerill stabbed a rebound high.

Afterwards a jubilant Allen Batsford declared: 'I knew a win would come our way sooner or later. The lads worked very hard and I'm very pleased. We have dominated matches before this season but still lost'. They followed up the win with another, three days later against Newport, which left the Club in 20th place with seven points from nine games.

The win left two Wimbledon stalwarts with distinctly mixed feelings. First Roger Connell, the big striker who had shaved off his beard for League football, watched the game from the dug-out as his replacement Summerill became the hero of the hour. It was Connell's poor form that had prompted Batsford to swoop for the Millwall striker.

Secondly, Dickie Guy watched his sixth game from the stands as his usurper, Richard Teale, had an awkward game. He came under no sustained pressure but made important saves whenever there was danger.

Time was on their side. By November both Guy and Connell were back in the side. Connell was destined to end the season as top scorer; Guy faced further competition following the arrival of another Millwall man — Ray Goddard — in January. It was a battle Goddard won.

WIMBLEDON: Teale, Tilley, Galvin, Bryant, Edwards, Bassett, Galliers, Davies, Summerill, Holmes, Leslie. Sub: Connell (Not Used).
NORTHAMPTON TOWN: Garnham, Tucker, Mead, Liddle, Litt, Bryant, Farrington, Williams (Best), Riley, Martin, McGowan.
CROWD: 3,326 REFEREE: A. Tarvey (Hants)

26th November 1977: FA CUP 1st ROUND
Enfield 3 *Knapman, Bass, O'Sullivan*
Wimbledon 0

Allen Batsford must have known his reign as Wimbledon manager was coming to an end after this dismal Cup defeat. Although he caried on for seven more games, and saw the Dons through the Christmas period, he resigned days after a 3-0 defeat at Swansea on 2 January.

Defeat at Isthmian League Enfield, a side Wimbledon would have expected to beat comfortably 12 months earlier, came in the middle of a poor run, that edged Batsford's men into the re-election zone. It was confidence, or rather the lack of it, which beat the Dons at Southberry Road.

Enfield were never three goals better than Wimbledon but they took their chances well and in the end deserved their victory. For the Dons, defeat gave them the chance 'to concentrate on the League' but it was clear in the grim weeks that followed that any diversion would have been helpful.

Dons started well enough, Phil Summerill and Geoff Davies pushing forward up front while at the back Dave Donaldson and Dave Galvin effectively snuffed out danger man Tony Bass and goal crony John Bishop. But in the 38th minute John Knapman broke the deadlock when he converted a Bishop pass and Enfield never looked back.

After the break the Dons were unable to impose themselves on the match, despite the efforts of John Leslie. The lively wingman created a number of chances down the left-hand side which were wasted due to lack of support.

Steve Galliers was brought in on the hour, presumably to inject some pace into midfield which looked laboured and slow. It was three minutes after his arrival that Bass scored the killer second goal. Galliers could not be faulted; indeed it took a superb header from the target man to beat the diving Guy.

The match was wrapped up with only eight minutes remaining, when Keith Elley's cross left Dickie Guy stranded and Micky O'Sullivan scored with ease. It completed a sad afternoon for the disappointing Dons.

Allen Batsford was outwardly calm after the match, praising the team's approach. 'I was quite happy with the way we were playing up until the time Enfield got their first goal,' he said. 'We were organised and showed plenty of fire but we did not show enough threat up front due to the lack of the right striker, namely the injured Roger Connell.'

He continued: 'Phil Summerill and Paul Denny did a fine job but they are too similar in their style. That's why I moved Geoff Davies forward and brought in Steve Galliers later on. I thought Enfield lacked pace myself and they certainly posed no surprise for us. We matched them well during the early stages'.

It was the FA Cup that had brought Batsford's team to prominence in previous years. A heavy defeat at Enfield, supposedly much weaker than the Dons, could only sound warning bells for the manager.

Batsford certainly hit the nail on the head when he summed up by saying: 'Winning used to be a habit for us and now we've lost it. We must start to cultivate that habit again'. Winning ways would return but only after Batsford had gone and his young assistant — Dario Gradi — had taken his place.

ENFIELD: Moore, Wright, Elley, Jennings, Tone, Howell, O'Sullivan, Knapman, Bishop, Bass, Searle. Sub: Glover (not used).
WIMBLEDON: Guy, Bryant, Galvin, Donaldson, Eames, Bassett, Aitken, Davies, Summerill, Denny (Galliers 68 mins), Leslie.
CROWD: 2,826 REFEREE: Mr A. Porter (Bolton)

27 March 1978: FOOTBALL LEAGUE DIVISION FOUR
Wimbledon 5 *Cork 2, Leslie, Bryant, Parsons*
Rochdale 1 *Scaife*

Confirmation of the transformation that Dario Gradi had achieved in under three months in charge came with this result. Almost exactly three months earlier, Batsford's Dons had crashed 3-0 to bottom-of-the-table Rochdale at Spotland on a miserable Boxing Day. With only five men surviving from that encounter, Wimbledon crushed the Lancashire side, visiting Plough Lane for the first time, with a brilliant display.

Before the match the current form table in the national newspaper showed that over the last 10 games Wimbledon had produced promotion form. Only Southend, Watford and Aldershot — all pushing for a place in Division Three — were playing better. Gradi was pleased with how his side was gelling together, but under no illusion about his main priority. He commented: 'I reckon we need a point a game for the rest of the season to avoid re-election'.

He knew that if they failed to gain the necessary points, the Club would become the first to apply for re-election in their first League season for over forty years. But Gradi was buoyant and was thinking long-term as he made clear when he said: 'I'm very pleased with the way we are playing. If we continue like this we must be good bets for promotion next season. The players are now more confident and we must be in with a good chance of surviving'.

The reason for his optimism was clear. He had blended together old campaigners like Ray Goddard and Dave Galvin with young tyros such as Alan Cork and Steve Parsons, to make a formidable team. The side was playing with a confidence and style unthinkable just weeks before. This win was the first half of an Easter double; four points which moved the Dons well away from the re-election places.

It was Alan Cork who opened the scoring after just 11 minutes, following up after goalkeeper Slack could not hold his first effort. The Dons then had to ride out a frustrating period, during which they could not make any impression in midfield against an enthusiastic Rochdale side. The zenith of Rochdale's achievements came in a crazy goalmouth scramble midway through the first half. Ray Goddard saved at least four shots as the Dons' defence found it impossible to clear their lines.

At the other end, the Dons were always high and wide with their chances, until they made it 2-0 in the 44th minute. John Leslie broke clear with two men shadowing him, and ran wide of Slack to score from an acute angle on the right with Roger Connell sliding in to make sure.

Rochdale showed that they had not given up the fight by scoring soon after the restart. Wimbledon's defence was stretched and Bobby Scaife headed a 47th minute goal. This spurred on the Dons, who had several more chances before a superb third from Jeff Bryant in the 62nd minute. Bryant ghosted in from the left to meet Steve Parsons' free kick from the right with a beautifully timed glancing header.

Connell headed over a Leslie cross before he set up Cork for the fourth. He dragged back from the right after a long ball from Galvin found him clear and Cork side-footed home with six minutes left. Steve Parsons completed the scoring in injury time with the fifth from a rebound.

Commenting after the game, Gradi was buoyant: 'We were very organised against Rochdale. We're dangerous and hard to beat and can compete with anyone'.

WIMBLEDON: Goddard, Bryant, Bradley, Briley, Galvin, Donaldson, Leslie, Denny, Connell, Cork, Parsons. Sub: Galliers (not used).

ROCHDALE: Slack, Hallows, Oliver, Morrin, Scott, Bannon, Scaife, O'Loughlin, Esser, Owen, Tarbuck.

CROWD: 2,737 REFEREE: Mr B. Daniels (Essex)

Billy Holmes shoots for goal in the first half against Northampton Town.

ABOVE: Phil Summerill scores on his debut as he notches Dons' second against Northampton. BELOW: Phil Summerill heads just wide against Enfield in the FA Cup.

ABOVE: Roger Connell shrugs off Rochdale's Banman. BELOW: Alan Cork pops in the Dons' fourth goal through the legs of Rochdale's Bob Scott.

1977 - 78 AT A GLANCE

DATE	OPPONENTS	H/A	Res.	Att.	1	2	3	4	5	6	7	8	9	10	11	12
Aug.13	Gillingham (FLC)	A	1-1	3,868	Guy	Tilley	Bryant	Donaldson	Edwards	Bassett	Galliers	Smith	Connell	Holmes 1	Leslie	Aitken
16	Gillingham (FLC)	H	3-1	3,784	Guy	Tilley	Bryant	Donaldson	Edwards	Bassett 1	Galliers	Smith	Connell 1	Holmes 1	Leslie	Davies (9)
20	Halifax Town	H	3-3	4,616	Guy	Bryant	Galvin	Donaldson	Aitken	Davies	Galliers	Smith	Connell 1	Holmes	Leslie 1	Eames
22	Brentford	A	1-4	11,001	Guy	Tilley	Bryant 1	Donaldson	Aitken	Davies	Galliers	Smith	Connell	Holmes	Leslie	Galvin
27	Torquay United	A	1-1	4,162	Teale	Tilley	Bryant	Donaldson	Edwards	Bassett	Galliers	Davies	Connell 1	Holmes	Aitken	Leslie (7)
31	Tottenham. H. (FU)	A	0-4	22,807	Teale	Tilley	Bryant	Donaldson	Edwards	Bassett	Galliers	Davies	Connell	Holmes	Aitken	Leslie (7)
Sept. 3	Southport	H	2-2	3,606	Teale	Tilley	Bryant	Donaldson	Edwards 1	Bassett	Aitken	Davies	Connell	Holmes	Leslie	Galliers
10	Hartlepool	A	0-3	2,709	Teale	Bryant	Galvin	Donaldson	Edwards	Bassett	Aitken	Davies	Connell	Holmes	Denny	Galliers
13	Aldershot	H	1-2	4,446	Teale	Bryant	Galvin	Donaldson	Edwards 1	Bassett	Aitken	Galliers	Davies	Holmes	Leslie	Denny
17	Scunthorpe United	A	0-3	2,618	Teale	Bryant	Galvin	Donaldson	Edwards	Bassett	Aitken	Galliers	Davies	Holmes	Leslie	Connell (4)
24	Northampton Town	H	2-0	3,236	Teale	Tilley	Galvin	Bryant	Edwards	Bassett	Galliers	Davies	Summerill 1	Holmes 1	Leslie	Connell
27	Newport County	H	3-0	3,941	Teale	Tilley	Galvin 1	Bryant	Edwards	Bassett	Galliers	Davies 1	Summerill	Holmes 1	Leslie	Connell
Oct.1	Reading	A	2-2	4,369	Teale	Tilley	Galvin	Bryant	Edwards	Bassett	Galliers	Davies	Summerill 1	Holmes 1	Leslie	Connell
4	Grimsby Town	A	1-3	4,048	Teale	Tilley	Galvin	Bryant	Edwards	Bassett	Galliers	Davies	Summerill 1	Holmes	Aitken	Connell
8	Crewe Alexandra	H	0-0	2,634	Teale	Tilley	Galvin	Bryant	Edwards	Bassett	Galliers	Davies	Summerill	Holmes	Leslie	Connell
15	A.F.C. Bournemouth	A	2-1	4,272	Teale	Tilley	Galvin	Bryant	Edwards	Bassett	Galliers	Davies	Summerill	Holmes 1	Leslie 1	Aitken
22	Southend United	H	1-3	4,448	Teale	Tilley	Galvin 1	Bryant	Edwards	Bassett	Galliers	Davies	Summerill	Holmes	Leslie	Connell
25	Dartford (SLCC)	H	3-2	986	Guy	Bryant	Galvin	Donaldson	Edwards	Bassett	Galliers 1	Davies 1	Connell 1	Holmes	Leslie	Aitken
29	Darlington	A	1-3	2,710	Teale	Bryant	Edwards	Donaldson	Galvin	Bassett	Galliers	Davies	Summerill	Holmes 1	Leslie	Aitken
Nov. 5	Swansea City	H	1-1	2,701	Teale	Bryant	Galvin	Donaldson	Edwards	Bassett	Aitken	Davies	Summerill 1	Connell	Leslie	Galliers (7)
7	Darlington	H	1-1	2,028	Teale	Bryant	Galvin	Donaldson	Edwards	Bassett	Aitken 1	Davies	Summerill	Connell	Leslie	Galliers
19	York City	H	2-1	2,056	Guy	Bryant	Galvin	Donaldson	Edwards	Bassett	Aitken	Davies	Summerill	Connell	Leslie 2	Galliers (10)
26	Enfield (FAC)	A	0-3	2,849	Guy	Bryant	Galvin	Donaldson	Eames	Bassett	Aitken	Davies	Summerill	Denny	Leslie	Galliers (10)
Dec. 2	Stockport County	A	2-2	5,008	Guy	Tilley	Galvin	Donaldson	Eames	Bassett	Galliers	Davies	Summerill	Denny 1	Leslie 2	Aitken
6	Boston. U. (NPL/SLC C)	H	1-1	646	Guy	Tilley	Bryant	Donaldson	Eames	Bassett	Galliers	Davies	Summerill	Denny	Leslie	Parsons
10	Barnsley	H	0-0	2,406	Guy	Bryant	Galvin	Donaldson	Eames	Bassett	Galliers	Davies	Summerill	Connell	Leslie	Denny
14	Boston. U. (NPL/SLC C)	A	0-1	1,550	Guy	Bryant	Galvin	Donaldson	Eames	Denny	Galliers	Davies	Summerill	Connell	Leslie	Parsons
17	Huddersfield Town	A	0-3	3,544	Guy	Bryant	Galvin	Donaldson	Edwards	Bassett	Galliers	Davies	Summerill	Connell	Leslie	Denny
26	Rochdale	A	0-3	1,248	Guy	Bryant	Galvin	Donaldson	Edwards	Bassett	Bithell	Davies	Summerill	Parsons	Leslie	Denny (8)
28	Doncaster Rovers	H	3-3	5,032	Guy	Bryant	Galvin	Donaldson	Edwards	Bassett	Galliers 1	Denny	Summerill	Parsons 1	Leslie 1	Davies
31	Watford	H	1-3	7,234	Guy	Bryant	Galvin	Donaldson	Edwards 1	Bassett	Galliers	Denny	Summerill	Parsons	Leslie	Davies
Jan. 2	Swansea City	A	0-3	9,700	Guy	Bassett	Bryant	Donaldson	Edwards	Davies	Galliers	Denny	Summerill	Parsons	Leslie	Eames
7	Brentford	H	1-1	5,411	Guy	Bryant	Galvin 1	Donaldson	Bithell	Bassett	Galliers	Denny	Summerill	Parsons	Leslie	Tilley
14	Halifax Town	A	2-1	2,770	Guy	Bryant 1	Galvin	Donaldson	Bithell	Bassett	Galliers	Denny 1	Summerill	Parsons	Edwards	Tilley (5)
21	Torquay United	H	0-1	2,300	Guy	Bithell	Bryant	Donaldson	Eames	Bassett	Galliers	Denny	Summerill	Parsons	Leslie	Tilley (2)
Feb. 11	Scunthorpe United	H	0-0	1,600	Goddard	Bithell	Eames	Galvin	Donaldson	Bassett	Leslie	Denny	Connell	Parsons	Cork	Galliers (7)
20	Hartlepool United	H	3-0	1,440	Goddard	Bryant	Eames	Denny	Galvin 2	Donaldson	Leslie	Bassett	Connell 1	Cork	Parsons	Summerill

Mar. 4 Crewe Alexandra	A	0-0	[illegible]	Goddard	Bryant	Eames	Denny	Galvin	Donaldson	Leslie	Bassett	Connell	Cork	Parsons	Briley [illegible]
8 Aldershot	A	1-3	4,632	Goddard	Bryant	Eames	Briley	Galvin	Bradley	Leslie	Bassett	Connell	Summerill	Parsons	Denny (3)
11 AFC Bournemouth	H	3-1	2,834	Goddard	Bryant	Bradley	Briley	Galvin	Donaldson	Leslie 1	Denny	Connell 1	Cork 1	Parsons	Summerill
17 Southend United	A	0-1	7,120	Goddard	Bryant	Bradley	Briley	Galvin	Donaldson	Leslie	Denny	Connell	Cork	Parsons	Summerill (2)
25 Doncaster Rovers	A	2-0	2,484	Goddard	Bryant 1	Bradley	Briley	Galvin	Donaldson	Leslie	Denny	Connell	Cork 1	Parsons	Eames
27 Rochdale	H	5-1	2,737	Goddard	Bryant 1	Bradley	Briley	Galvin	Donaldson	Leslie 1	Denny	Connell	Cork 2	Parsons 1	Galliers
Apr. 1 Watford	A	0-2	11,212	Goddard	Bryant	Eames	Briley	Galvin	Donaldson	Denny	Bassett	Connell	Cork	Parsons	Galliers (8)
4 Grimsby Town	H	2-2	2,380	Goddard	Bryant	Eames	Briley	Galvin	Donaldson	Leslie 1	Denny	Connell	Cork	Parsons 1	Bassett
8 Huddersfield Town	H	2-0	2,602	Goddard	Bryant 1	Eames	Briley	Galvin	Donaldson	Leslie 1	Denny	Connell	Cork	Parsons	Bassett
15 York City	A	1-1	1,617	Goddard	Bryant	Eames	Galvin	Donaldson	Briley	Leslie	Denny	Connell 1	Cork	Parsons	Galliers (8)
17 Southport	A	5-0	1,604	Goddard	Bryant 1	Eames	Briley	Galvin	Donaldson	Leslie 1	Bassett	Connell 2	Cork	Parsons 1	Bradley
22 Stockport County	H	2-0	2,763	Goddard	Bryant	Eames	Briley 1	Galvin	Donaldson	Leslie 1	Bassett	Connell	Cork	Parsons	Denny
25 Newport County	A	1-0	2,112	Goddard	Bryant	Eames	Briley	Bradley	Donaldson	Cowley	Denny	Connell 1	Cork	Parsons	Bassett
29 Barnsley	A	2-3	2,479	Goddard	Bradley	Eames	Briley	Galvin	Donaldson	Leslie	Denny	Connell 2	Cork	Cowley	Bryant

FINAL TABLE

LEAGUE DIVISION FOUR

	P	W	D	L	F	A	W	D	L	F	A	Pts
Watford	46	18	4	1	44	14	12	7	4	41	24	71
Southend	46	15	5	3	46	18	10	5	8	20	21	60
Swansea	46	16	5	2	54	17	7	5	11	33	30	56
Brentford	46	15	6	2	50	17	6	8	9	36	37	56
Aldershot	46	15	8	0	45	16	4	8	11	22	31	54
Grimsby	46	14	6	3	30	15	7	5	11	27	36	53
Barnsley	46	15	4	4	44	20	3	10	10	17	29	50
Reading	46	12	7	4	33	23	6	7	10	22	29	50
Torquay	46	12	6	5	43	25	4	9	10	14	31	47
Northampton	46	9	8	6	32	30	8	5	10	31	38	47
Huddersfield	46	13	5	5	41	21	2	10	11	22	34	45
Doncaster	46	11	8	4	37	26	3	9	11	15	39	45
WIMBLEDON	46	8	11	4	39	26	6	5	12	27	41	44
Scunthorpe	46	12	6	5	31	14	2	10	11	19	41	44
Crewe	46	11	8	4	34	25	4	6	13	16	44	44
Newport	46	14	6	3	43	22	2	5	16	22	51	43
Bournemouth	46	12	6	5	28	20	2	9	12	13	31	43
Stockport	46	14	4	5	41	19	2	6	15	15	37	42
Darlington	46	10	8	5	31	22	4	5	14	21	37	41
Halifax	46	7	10	6	28	23	3	11	9	24	39	41
Hartlepool	46	12	4	7	34	29	3	3	17	17	55	37
York	46	8	7	8	27	31	4	5	14	23	38	36
Southport	46	5	13	5	30	32	1	6	16	22	44	31
Rochdale	46	8	6	9	29	28	0	2	21	14	57	24

GOALS AND GAMES

APPEARANCES AND GOALSCORERS

	Appearances			Goals	
	Lge	Cup	Sub	Lge	Cup
Glenn Aitken	11	2		1	
Dave Bassett	35	4			1
Brian Bithell	6				
Dave Bradley	7				
Les Briley	13		1	1	
Jeff Bryant	43	4		7	
Roger Connell	28	3	2	14	2
Alan Cork	17			4	
Fran Cowley	2			4	
Geoff Davies	23	2		2	1
Paul Denny	23	1	3	1	1
Dave Donaldson	38	4			
Terry Eames	17	1	1		
Billy Edwards	21	3		2	
Steve Galliers	22	3	5	1	1
Dave Galvin	40	1		5	
Ray Goddard	18	5	2	6	
Dickie Guy	13	3		5	2
Billy Holmes	15	3		5	2
John Leslie	40	3	1	13	
Steve Parsons	24			5	
Willie Smith	2	2			
Phil Summerill	22	1	2	4	1
Richard Teale	15	1			
Kevin Tilley	11	3	2		

Wimbledon 1977-78. Back row: Dario Gradi (Manager), Dave Donaldson, Paul Denny, Jeff Bryant, Dickie Guy, Geoff Davies, Roger Connell, Phil Summerill, Steve Parsons. Front row: Brian Bithell, Dave Bassett, John Leslie, Steve Galliers, Kevin Tilley and Terry Eames.

ABOVE: Aldershot's Murray Brodie challenges Roy Goddard for the ball during the opening day game at the Recreation Ground. BELOW: Jeff Bryant (centre) glances his header just wide against Northampton as John Leslie and Roger Connell wait.

Gradi's Youngsters Race to Promotion 1978-79

Unbeaten run to the top

Wimbledon began the 1978-79 season with only one aim — promotion. Dario Gradi completely reorganised pre-season training to ensure that his side was ready to face a gruelling 46 match League programme. 'Last season's preparation was not satisfactory, quite frankly,' he commented in August. 'This time everything has been done properly and our week away in the West Country was just what we needed.'

He continued: 'Promotion will naturally be our prime target and I will obviously be disappointed if we don't make it. Injury will be a key factor and we have been lucky that no-one has been injured during training. However, it we don't get up, I don't think I personally will have failed'.

The only new face in the squad was Ray Knowles, signed for £2,000 from non-League Southall. In the Boardroom, long-serving director John Reid retired along with former England cricket captain Tony Greig. New skipper Les Briley was as buoyant as Gradi, commenting: 'Everybody at the Club thinks we have a great chance of winning promotion this time. Confidence is high and that can only be a good thing for the Club'.

Wimbledon's first friendly was against Colchester on 25 July and the Third Division side were beaten 2-0 at Plough Lane. The Dons then spent a week at Exeter University, building up fitness, and managed wins at Bideford (4-1) and Dawlish (2-1) during their stay. They returned to London during the second week of August and beat a Malawi International XI 5-0 — with Alan Cork grabbing a hat-trick — before 2nd Division Crystal Palace administered a 5-0 reverse to deflate any swelling egos.

Chairman Ron Noades underlined the ambition about the Club. 'There is a 10-year plan pinned to the office wall. Last year was for ground improvements; this year for things on the field. We have been surprised at the way things have gone, but we have the right spirit here. Everyone works . . . directors, committee, staff, players. We still have our non-League attitudes off the pitch in the way we graft to raise money and run the Club. But on the field we are as professional as anyone.'

Assistant manager, Dave Bassett, epitomised the keenness that has always been a feature of Wimbledon FC. 'What we have now is a team of young players who are just grateful for being in the League and playing football. That gratefulness shows in everything they do. They are full of enthusiasm. They want to get on. They rush back for extra training in the afternoons. There are no lame ducks here; no players just in it for the pay packet. If anyone showed the wrong attitude he would be kicked out in no time.'

Bassett continued: 'The lads have been given every opportunity and they have grabbed it. Who knows how far we can go? The First Division must be our ultimate aim. We are all so involved we could go all the way . . .'. Prophetic words indeed!

The season began at promoted Southend in the League Cup. The Dons matched the Third Division side in all departments and were only beaten by an unlucky Dave Galvin own goal. In the second leg the following Tuesday, Wimbledon overturned the deficit in style, winning 4-1. The damage was done by three goals in seven minutes — from Paul Denny, Steve Galliers and Alan Cork — just before half time.

That was the prelude to a devastating thirteen match unbeaten League run which sent the Dons to the top of Division 4 for the first time in their history. Quoted at 4 to 1 for promotion, they looked good odds after an opening day point at much fancied Aldershot. Wimbledon's first League goal of the season was scored by Jeff Bryant — just as it had been twelve months earlier.

Relegated Port Vale were at Plough Lane for the initial home game and returned to the Potteries defeated by the only goal — a lazy curling chip from Alan Cork. The next visitors, Northampton Town, must have been fed up with Wimbledon as they crashed 4-1; their third defeat in twelve months against the South Londoners. Alan Cork took his personal tally to four goals in three games with the first-ever Football League hat-trick by a Dons player.

In the League Cup 2nd Round, the Dons were again drawn away to a 1st Division side. Twelve months earlier it had been Spurs; this time they made the journey to Goodison Park. It was a memorable occasion for all the wrong reasons as five goals from Bob Latchford and three from Martin Dobson led to a record 8-0 defeat. Unperturbed, Wimbledon returned to the North West three nights later for their next League match against Stockport County. An Alan Cork goal secured the win to make it seven points out of eight for Gradi's side.

Most of the team now had a settled look about it with Goddard in goal, Jeff Bryant and Terry Eames the full backs, Donaldson and Galvin the centre back pairing, and a midfield of Galliers, Briley and John Leslie. However, up front Alan Cork was the only regular with Roger Connell, Paul Denny, Phil Summerill and Steve Parsons competing for the other two spaces.

In the next match, League newcomers Wigan Athletic were beaten 2-1 at home, before the Dons surrendered a two goal lead at Blundell Park, Grimsby, with defender Jeff Bryant scoring at both ends. The draw left the Dons in second place with 10 points, below Barnsley only on goal difference. Boss Dario Gradi was pleased with the performance but disappointed not to win. 'It could easily have been two points but for Jeff's own goal. Everyone one was sick about that. On the other hand we played a brilliant game.'

Wimbledon travelled to Newport County the following week and came away with a 3-1 win which appeared more convincing that it was. After Rod Jones was sent off for kicking John Leslie, Wimbledon allowed Newport to take the lead with 15 minutes left. However, three late goals, including two from Leslie, saw them home.

It all set up a top-of-the-table clash between the two remaining unbeaten sides — Wimbledon and Reading. A crowd of over 5,000 turned out at Plough Lane on a beautiful late September day. One Alan Cork strike, from outside the box, settled the issue and, with Barnsley only able to draw, Wimbledon were top for the first time.

Dario Gradi was named *Evening Standard* Manager of the Month but refused to take most of the credit. 'It has been a real team effort,' he said. 'The players, mostly youngsters, have worked tremendously hard, the chairman Ron Noades has given me every conceivable help and we are now a full-time club with only Dave Donaldson, of our first team, part-time.'

ABOVE: Ray Goddard and Dave Galvin combine to foil Stockport County's Les Bradd at Edgeley Park. BELOW: Paul Denny fires this shot just over at home to Wigan Athletic.

ABVOVE: Ex-Don Dave Bradley and Paul Haverson challenge for this high ball in the home game with Doncaster Rovers. BELOW: Ray Knowles shoots wide under pressure in the top of the table clash at Barnsley.

Dons on course

The success and attention lifted the self-confidence of everyone at the Club. 'It's just fabulous to be top,' chirped assistant boss Dave Bassett after the Reading match. 'We all feel big, feel important — but in no way over-confident.' If anyone was getting arrogant their visit to Spotland, two days later, soon remedied that. Rochdale had not won all season and only a late penalty miss preserved the Dons' unbeaten record after they had been out-played.

But the Dons bounced back with three wins and a draw in their next four matches, to consolidate their position. Bradford City were beaten at home 2-1 before an excellent 4-1 win at York. Two home fixtures in four days then brought three points as Scunthorpe were dispatched 3-1 and Alan Cork's second half header secured a point against Crewe Alexandra.

The Crewe game saw only the second appearance as a substitute, of Fran Cowley. 'He has always had ability,' said Gradi, 'but so often lacked the end product. Tonight he produced it'. Cowley set up Steve Parsons for his 79th minute cross; Cork headed home.

The proud thirteen match unbeaten record ended when the injury-hit Dons lost 3-0 at Huddersfield. Dario Gradi complained that his squad was simply not big enough so he acted quickly, signing 19-year-old Paul Haverson and 23-year-old Steve Perkins, for a combined fee of £5,000, from QPR.

Both made immediate debuts as Wimbledon beat Doncaster 3-2 at home with Alan Cork netting his thirteenth goal of the season. His goals, and those of John Leslie, were helping to disguise an increasingly error-prone defence. The problems were shown up starkly the next Saturday as an 11,761 crowd at third-placed Barnsley saw Wimbledon beaten 3-1 and knocked off the top. The home manager called it his side's hardest test, but the Dons' cause was not helped when Jeff Bryant was sent off for arguing.

The first sign that the Club was not happy with their Plough Lane home was the announcement that Wimbledon and Fulham were looking to build a 30,000 all-seater stadium at St George's Playing Field in Raynes Park. Noades said: 'I don't want our facilities to be below top-class standard. The team is shaping up well and we believe there is demand for excellent surroundings angled towards the family in South London'. It was the opening salvo of a long-running battle with Merton Council.

The team, meanwhile, responded well to the defeat at Barnsley, by beating Stockport 2-0 with a brace from Paul Denny. The following week they travelled to Northampton and were held to 1-1 following a twice-taken penalty. Ray Goddard saved the first kick, from Steve Phillips, but had no chance with the second, taken by Tony Gedmintis, after the referee ruled he moved too soon.

The new stadium plan took another turn with the news that Surrey CC wanted to share the site. They were looking, like Fulham, to move south from their present site at the Oval, and sharing the costs of the £6 million sports complex looked attractive. Finding an area acceptable to the Council would prove more problematic.

Wimbledon had drawn Gravesend in the FA Cup and, after a 0-0 draw in Kent — in which Steve Parsons had a penalty saved twice — an Alan Cork header settled the replay deep into extra time. Two more from Cork saw off Halifax at home before a Paul Denny goal secured a point from the long journey to Hartlepool.

The Dons — who had recently welcomed back Les Briley after a long injury — were back on top of the table. With 20 matches of a long campaign completed they had every reason to be pleased with themselves.

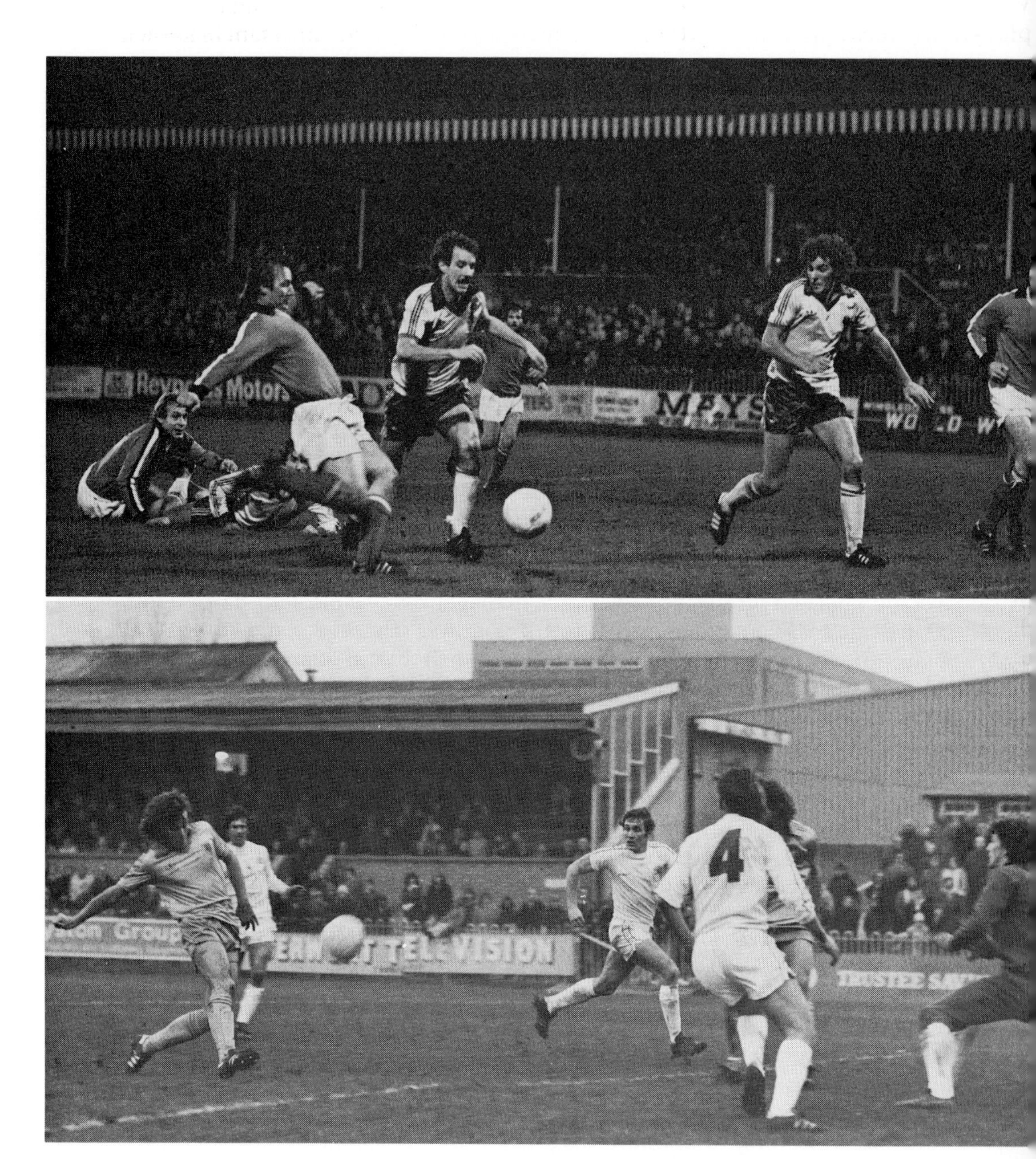

ABOVE: Alan Cork and Paul Denny break through in the FA Cup replay at Gravesend. BELOW: Paul Denny lifts his volley over the bar at home to Halifax Town.

South Coast blues

Having spent the season travelling back and forwards to the north of England, Wimbledon faced five games with South Coast clubs over the Christmas and New Year period. And what crucial games they were, each one exciting and important in its own right.

The FA Cup 2nd Round draw had brought AFC Bournemouth to Plough Lane. Only a second half equaliser from Paul Denny had stopped the Dons going out after Ted McDougall's early goal. Wimbledon were fortunate to survive as Ray Goddard made a string of fine saves.

The replay should have been four days later but bad weather caused a late postponement, after the coaches carrying the Wimbledon supporters had arrived at Dean Court. By coincidence the Dons were in Bournemouth again that Saturday – this time for a League game. An improved performance and goals from Steve Galliers and Paul Denny set up a 2-1 win. The two points maintained their lead in the Championship chase.

Boxing Day 1978 brought Portsmouth to Plough Lane. The first v third clash attracted 8,000 fans of whom around half had travelled from the South Coast. The structural inadequacies of the ground were shown up, as non-existent segregation allowed the away fans to roam around the terraces at will and fencing collapsed behind one goal. Soon after that match the home and away terraces were segregated and the practice of changing ends at half time stopped. The 'Pompey Chimes' could be heard all over SW19 after Portsmouth's 4-2 win, despite the Dons leading 2-1 at half time.

Two days later the team returned to Dean Court as a 7,000 crowd, swelled by the prospect of a 3rd Round tie with Southampton, were silenced by a brilliant Dons display. Ted MacDougall once again gave Bournemouth the lead but Steve Parsons set up Cork for an 88th minute equalizer. Ray Goddard held out against fierce home pressure in extra time before Steve Parsons scored direct from a corner with only minutes remaining. 'That was the most nerve-tingling game I've ever seen,' admitted Gradi afterwards. 'My body's still shaking but isn't it tremendous!'

The 3rd Round tie against 1st Division Southampton was postponed on Saturday 6 January because the pitch was covered with snow. Schoolboy volunteers cleared most of the pitch, but it was to no avail as the ground below was frozen. By Tuesday night it had thawed enough for the match to go ahead in front of a disappointing 9,000 crowd. Wimbledon missed crucial early chances and bowed out, following two Phil Boyer strikes.

There were no more matches in January due to continued bad weather and only three were played in February. Lowly Rochdale were beaten on the 3rd by three goals to two and then long trips to Wigan on the 14th and Torquay on the 28th both yielded maximum points. The Torquay match was remarkable in that Wimbledon won 6-1 and Alan Cork scored four. He was now the Division's leading goal scorer and rumours began to circulate about his departure to a bigger club.

As always finance was high on the Club's agenda. Low crowds were a major concern, with the average increasing only slightly despite the top-of-the-table position. Friday night soccer was discussed but rejected because it would clash with greyhound racing at the neighbouring Wimbledon Stadium.

But Chairman Noades was ringing no alarm bells over a cash crisis. Speaking at the end of February he commented: 'It's really only a short-term cashflow problem. We are in quite a good position financially and we're not that worried'. Wimbledon had played only three times in 56 days and had suffered eight cancellations due to the weather. Their weekly wage bill was around £2,500.

Noades explained that he had just received £10,000 from the Football League. The money came from a four per cent levy imposed on all League clubs' gate receipts. Normally it was distributed at the end of the season but, due to the freeze-up, it was handed out a few months early. Long term, there were plans for up to 900 more seats, in the North and South Stands. A restaurant to link up with the Sportsman Pub was another idea.

In the short term, Wimbledon continued to focus on their one aim — Division Three. The big freeze had affected them more than other clubs and, although still well placed, they faced a demanding final three months of the season.

ABOVE: Jeff Bryant is beaten to the cross by Bournemouth goalkeeper Kenny Allen in the FA Cup-tie at Plough Lane. BELOW: Alan Cork's shot is blocked by Pompey's full back Billy Wilson in the Boxing Day thriller.

ABOVE: Southampton goalie Terry Glennoe wins this chase for the ball with Steve Parsons in the FA Cup 3rd Round tie. BELOW: Steve Parsons lifts this chance over the bar during the 3-2 win over Rochdale.

ABOVE: Paul Denny and Jeff Bryant are grounded but the ball flies wide against Huddersfield Town. BELOW: Paul Haverson scores from the spot at home to Aldershot.

The long run-in

By the time the Dons were able to play regularly again it was March and there were only twelve weeks of the season left. Twenty-one matches still had to be played and all their promotion rivals had played three or four games more. Despite this, only Reading had moved ahead with 38 points from 28 games to 36 from 24 for Wimbledon.

On 3 March the Dons began a run-in which was to see them playing twice a week until the middle of May. Young Phil Driver, who had previously made only one substitute appearance, came off the bench for the second time and struck a wonderful volley five minutes from time, to secure the points against Huddersfield Town. Three days later Newport County were at the Lane and a defensive display ensured them a 0-0 draw.

A bizarre game at Doncaster followed which saw the Dons' title hopes dented. Trailing 1-0 to a first half Rovers' goal, the team were taken off during a second half blizzard. Sadly it cleared sufficiently for the match to finish in defeat. The slump continued with two more 1-0 defeats — at home to third-placed Grimsby and away to lowly Port Vale.

Despite having at least four games in hand on the teams above them, Wimbledon had dropped to fifth, but Dario Gradi remained confident after the match at Vale Park. 'Obviously it's a set-back, but it's nothing we can't put right,' he said. The main concern was the attack which had not scored for six hours.

Gradi's optimism was well founded as his team hit back at its critics with two wins in four days. A real four-pointer — in front of over 5,000 at Plough Lane — saw them outplay Aldershot to win 3-1 and that was followed by a 2-0 success against Hereford with marksmen John Leslie and Alan Cork finally back in the scoring frame.

With the transfer deadline approaching, Gradi acted to strengthen the defence. Tommy Cunningham was signed from QPR for a Club record £45,000 while fellow central defender Paul Bowgett was signed from Tottenham for a bargain £1,000. It was the end for three of the older members of the side. Dave Donaldson had been dropped before Christmas and he was followed out of the team by Jeff Bryant and Dave Galvin.

For the visit of Bournemouth the new-look defence was taking shape. In front of goalkeeper Ray Goddard were full-backs Haverson and Perkins, with Cunningham and Bowgett forming an imposing centre back pairing. It certainly did the trick, as the final ten games saw a miserly seven goals conceded.

Prior to beating the Cherries for the third time that season, this time by four goals to nil, the Dons had lost twice in Yorkshire — at Bradford and Halifax. Six visits to the County yielded only two points during the 1978-79 season. The match on Easter Saturday at Portsmouth led to a happer journey home. Two world-class Ray Goddard saves ensured a point in a goalless draw in front of over 11,000. Then, on the following Monday, visiting Torquay were outclassed again, this time by 5-0.

A point at Darlington and a win at Crewe pushed the team back into the four promotion places. Manager Dario Gradi made it clear after the 2-1 success at Gresty Road that he would accept no excuses now if his team failed to make the Third Division. 'It was a bonus to get two points,' he said. 'I believe we now have to get six points from seven games to make sure of promotion. If we don't do this, we deserve to be shot!'

Two of these points were secured, at home to a poor Hartlepool side, before the showdown with top-of-the-table Reading. Elm Park hosted over 13,000 to see an already promoted Royals team attempt to secure the title. Despite having more possession, the Dons had few goal attempts, and it was John Alexander who scored the only goal of the night for the home side.

The tension continued to show as visits to Hereford and Scunthorpe yielded a solitary point. Three more points were needed from three Plough Lane fixtures. They took place in a six day period and they made almost certain at the first attempt with a Friday night win over York. The young Dons' team showed their nerves by going behind to a York side with nothing to play for. But it was the Leslie-Cork partnership which finally secured two precious points. Alan Cork's winner came with only five minutes left and Wimbledon's fans poured onto the pitch to celebrate.

The point they needed, to guarantee Third Division football, came against Barnsley on Monday 14 May — two days after the Cup Final. A crowd of nearly six thousand, including 16 coachloads from Yorkshire, saw a tense encounter. The 1-1 draw left both sets of supporters to contemplate life in a higher League. Young Wally Downes, in only his second game, gave Wimbledon a first half lead, with Phil Chambers equalising late on.

Said Wimbledon manager Dario Gradi: 'I'm relieved, more than anything else, particularly for the players. The last few weeks have been very nerve-wracking. I feel as though I have just done a marathon. My initial feeling is one of relief'. Skipper Les Briley commented: 'It's been a long hard season and we've had our ups and downs, but not once did I ever think we wouldn't make it. We had to come through a bad winter, but we did it. We knew we were up on Friday night, but it was nice to make doubly sure on Monday. It was a good game. Barnsley are a good side, but we are better. We're young and can go a long way'.

It was Briley who collected the bubbly before the Dons' final match against Darlington, for winning the *Evening Standard's* champagne-for-goals contest. A 2-0 win left the team on 61 points and third in the table. Alan Cork's 22 goals made him the second highest scorer in the Division behind Aldershot's John Dungworth.

After the match Ron Noades outlined the plans for £140,000 worth of ground developments which would make the Plough Lane face-lift worth £330,000 since they joined the Football League. Wimbledon planned a bar in the South Stand, and to erect a youth club and day nursery. Behind the West Terrace an £80,000 all-weather surface was to be developed, so that facilities appealed to people of all ages. The Chairman commented: 'Our support is not very large yet but we are trying hard to improve it'.

Gradi was confident that on the pitch too the Club would match its higher station 'The Club already has players good enough to make their mark in a higher grade and I'm sure they will do just that'. He cited Wally Downes as an example of a young talent developing. 'That is what I mean when I say we have young players who have the ability and skill to make an impact.'

One interesting footnote: in his programme column for the Darlington match Gradi included thanks to Sam Hammam for his help during the season — a first public mention for a man who would loom large in the years ahead.

ABOVE: Ray Knowles is put under pressure by two Hereford defenders during the 0-0 home draw. BELOW: Steve Parsons lines up his shot at Elm Park as Reading's Gary Peters closes in.

ABOVE: Steve Death holds on under pressure from Wimbledon's Phil Summerill, Ray Knowles and Jeff Bryant. BELOW: John Leslie and Lawrie Sanchez challenge for the ball in the Reading match. Dave Donaldson keeps a watchful eye on proceedings.

Memorable Matches 1978-9

23 September 1978: FOOTBALL LEAGUE DIVISION FOUR
Wimbledon 1 *Cork*
Reading 0

A stunning goal from Alan Cork sent Wimbledon to the top of the 4th Division table for the first time in their history. The clash between the only two unbeaten sides in the Division attracted almost double the average attendance to Plough Lane, where fans saw an intriguing match between well-matched teams.

In glorious weather, both teams started cautiously probing from midfield without causing much danger to the respective defences. John Leslie was outstanding in midfield as he linked with Steve Galliers and Paul Denny to control the central area. Just before the interval Wimbledon nearly took the lead, when an accurate Knowles lob was cleared off the line by Bennett.

The second half started in much livelier fashion, with Wimbledon showing more urgency in attack. Phil Summerill got behind the Royals' defence on two occasions, but hurried finishing meant both chances were fired over.

After 70 minutes Cork picked up the ball 25 yards from goal and shrugged off two determined challenges before rifling home a searing shot from outside the box. It lifted Cork's personal tally for the season to nine and made him the Division's leading marksman.

The setback sparked the visitors into greater efforts to get back on terms. There was momentary danger for the Dons' defence, when Earles flashed a hard cross across the home goal, but no-one was available to apply the finishing touch.

The heat had now taken its toll of both sides and the final whistle came with the Dons comfortably holding on to their slender lead. Nineteen-year-old Cork was buoyant afterwards, declaring: 'I had a bet on that I'd get 15 this season but the way things are going I'll get that by Christmas'.

He was asked whether it had been a gamble to move from 1st Division Derby to the Dons. 'No, not really,' he replied. 'I just wanted to play first team football. My only worry was leaving home for the first time . . . now I don't really want to go back! It's terrific down here.'

Boss Dario Gradi, the man behind the Dons' change from a struggling outfit to a championship-chasing side, was unsurprisingly upbeat as he reflected on being top. 'It's a really nice feeling. Everyone wants to talk to you but I think the team should be getting all the publicity.'

When questioned on what was behind the current success he replied: 'It's the picking of lively players as opposed to established ones. The players that have been brought into the side have given it much more life and movement. All the younger ones have given a lot of enthusiasm. They have improved individually no end'.

Gradi stressed that the road ahead would be tough as only nine games had been played. Skipper Les Briley, who sat out the game as an injured spectator, was more confident. 'We have got to increase our lead at the top — not just hang on to it.'

The Reading side that day included two young men — Gary Peters and Lawrie Sanchez — who would have a great influence on the future of the Club in the years ahead. But that night the Dons were only interested in one thing, a League table which read:

	P	W	D	L	F	A	Pts
1 WIMBLEDON	8	6	2	0	15	6	14
2 Barnsley	8	6	1	1	11	7	13
3 Reading	8	5	2	1	12	4	12

WIMBLEDON: Goddard, Bryant, Eames, Galliers, Galvin, Donaldson, Leslie, Denny, Knowles (Parsons), Cork, Summerill.
READING: Death, Peters, White, Bowman, Hicks, Bennett, Earles, Hetzke, Kearns (Kearney), Sanchez, Lewis.
CROWD: 5,011 *REFEREE: Mr J. Hanting (Leics)*

26 December 1978: FOOTBALL LEAGUE DIVISION FOUR
Wimbledon 2 *Knowles 2*
Portsmouth 4 *Barnad, Davey, Wilson, Hemmermann*

Over 8,000 fans flocked to Plough Lane for this Boxing Day thriller. With both teams pushing hard for promotion, the stakes were high and neither side disappointed the holiday audience, in a match in which the lead changed hands several times.

There were only five minutes on the clock when Wimbledon went ahead, as Ray Knowles' side-footed the ball under the body of Peter Mellor in the Portsmouth goal. But the lead was short-lived and Leigh Barnard fired home an equaliser from 10 yards in the 11th minute.

Portsmouth, in their first-ever season in the basement section, had made steady progress up the League table after failing to win any of their opening five matches of the campaign. They were unbeaten, home or away, since late October, while Wimbledon had not lost at Plough Lane for nearly a year.

It was the Dons who eased in front on the stroke of half-time, when Knowles met a cross from the left with a low-driving header which beat the diving Mellor. But the holiday spirit was soured at half-time as railings collapsed behind the West Bank goal, while Portsmouth supporters surged around the terraces.

Within five minutes of the restart, Steve Davey had equalised and Pompey dominated from then on. A brilliant strike by Billy Wilson from 25 yards put the South Coast men in front and, when Jeff Hemmermann scored the fourth near the end, the points were safe. Indeed, it could have been worse, but for crucial saves from Ray Goddard.

At the end Wimbledon fans trooped home disappointed, to the deafening chorus of the *Pompey Chimes* ringing out again and again. The Dons' proud 20-match unbeaten home-run had ended, as Portsmouth drew up to within a point of Wimbledon at the top.

Manager Dario Gradi was not downhearted. In his programme notes for the next home match he wrote: 'Despite the result there was much to enjoy about the game. The pace and standard was above the average Fourth Division match. Just as we were getting on top we made two mistakes which gave them their second equaliser. Portsmouth are the best team I have seen so far this season'.

It was only the second game that season that centre back Dave Donaldson had missed. But although he was forced out through injury, Gradi decided it was time the 37-year-old finished his League career. He played only four more games for the Dons and was given a free transfer at the end of the season.

For Wimbledon it was the end of an era. Donaldson was the last part-time player on the staff of the Club. In the *Evening Standard* he described a typical day in his hectic 'double life':

9.30am	Begin journey to job No 1 — Wimbledon's training ground in Kingston Vale.
10.30am	Start training.
12.30pm	Finishing training and shower.
12.45pm	Change into airport uniform before a snack lunch in a nearby cafe.
2.30pm	Arrive at Heathrow. Start shift as a computer operator.
10.00pm	Finish shift.
10.30pm	Bed.

Donaldson, who was Player of the Year in 1976-77, was a crucial member of the side that won three successive Southern League Championships. With his departure the Club had become fully professional.

WIMBLEDON: Goddard, Bryant, Haverson, Galliers, Galvin, Eames, Leslie (Driver), Briley, Knowles, Cork, Cowley.

PORTSMOUTH: Mellor, Ellis, Viney, Denyer, Foster, Davey, Hemmermann, Latham, Wilson, Barnard, Pullar.

CROWD: 8,084 REFEREE: Mr B. Daniels (Essex)

9 January 1979: FA CUP 3rd ROUND
Wimbledon 0
Southampton 2 *Boyer 2*

Ignore the scoreline — Wimbledon could so easily have been giantkillers once again. All they had to do was put away the chances they had been gobbling up all season in the League and they would have beaten Southampton. However, nerves got the better of them at crucial moments and they went down to a side many supporters could not believe was in Division One.

The snow, which had caused the postponement of the tie the previous Saturday, cleared in time for the contest. It was Wimbledon who were first to take control of the vital midfield territory and in the first half-hour Cork, Parsons and Ketteridge all missed chances. Paul Denny went closest in the 33rd minute when his header shaved the bar with Gennoe beaten.

Southampton came back towards the end of the half and troubled the Dons' defence with some clever play down the wings. Each time the danger was cleared by a backline superbly marshalled by Ray Goddard. But it was a Goddard error that led to the opening goal in the 49th minute. Terry Curran crossed a ball that Goddard inexplicably ignored and Phil Boyer slid in at the far post to score.

Wimbledon brought on substitute John Leslie for the fading Ray Knowles and he made an immediate impact. His header beat Gennoe in the 72nd minute but was ruled out for handball. How times change! It was only eighteen months since the Saints goalkeeper had been on view for Halifax in Wimbledon's first League match. Now he returned a First Division player.

The Dons kept going forward and were always in with a chance of forcing a replay, until Boyer volleyed the tie beyond doubt with only minutes remaining. The result certainly flattered Southampton but a philosophical Gradi summed it when he said: 'You don't get many chances to score against a First Division side and we missed out when we failed to take ours at the start'.

He went on: 'It was a naive error that let in Southampton for the first goal, but it is an error that has since been corrected. We nullified their threats and had the chance to take the initiative but we let them in through our own basic mistakes. We still had enough chances to win it and Southampton manager Lawrie McMenemy said he would have settled for a draw'.

Some consolation for the Dons came in the form of record receipts from the 9,254 crowd. However, the number of people highlighted the sort of problems the Club would face if it fulfilled its ambition of reaching the First Division. Chairman Noades commented: 'We aim to be in the First Division by our centenary in 10 years' time, so everything we are doing is for the future'.

He revealed that the Club had plans before Merton Council that would turn Plough Lane into a 20,000 all-seater stadium. But he expressed concerns that, as the side gained promotion to higher divisions, the crowds and traffic would jam the streets around the ground.

'We are looking 10 years ahead and are planning a 30,000 all-seater stadium and sports complex,' Noades indicated. The plan involved buying a 42 acre site at Prince George's playing fields in Bushey Drive. Sadly Merton Council blocked the move at an early stage.

WIMBLEDON: Goddard, Perkins, Eames, Ketteridge, Galvin, Denny, Parsons, Briley, Knowles (Leslie), Cork, Haverson.
SOUTHAMPTON: Gennoe, Golac, Peach, Williams, Nicholl, Waldron, Ball, Boyer, Hebberd, Holmes, Curran.
CROWD: 9,254 REFEREE: Mr A. Glasson (Salisbury)

11 May 1979: FOOTBALL LEAGUE DIVISION 4
Wimbledon 2 *Leslie, Cork*
York City 1 *Ford*

Wimbledon were the toast of London after this win. Not only did the points virtually ensure Third Division football; it also meant the Dons topped the Capital scoring stakes. That earned them first prize in the *Evening News* champagne goals competition which meant each of the 21 men used in the promotion campaign qualified for six magnums of bubbly.

Meanwhile manager Dario Gradi was adamant that his young side would not sit back in the Third Division and just enjoy it. 'We have got the players good enough to impress and I'm sure we will,' he said. 'There will be a lot of players vying for position next term.' With a number of old-stagers offered free transfers, the accent was clearly on youth.

It was one of Gradi's youngsters — Alan Cork — who fired Wimbledon to promotion with his 25th goal of the season. His winner meant that Aldershot had only the slimmest mathematical chance of ousting the Dons from their promotional pedestal. That possibility was dismissed as jubilant Dons supporters swarmed onto the pitch at the end.

Yet the result might have been so different had mid-table York taken the best of their chances. Ahead after 35 minutes, when Gary Ford fired home a glorious goal from fully 30 yards out, they could have gone on to wrap up the points. The Dons' anxiety showed as they made mistakes throughout the first half.

Wimbledon breathed again and, with the excitement mounting, roared back to equalise soon after the restart. Steve Ketteridge crossed for John Leslie to sidefoot home in the 62nd minute. From then on a visibly more relaxed Dons side dominated the proceedings.

But it took Cork until five minutes from time to provide the moment all the supporters had been waiting for. He launched himself at a Steve Parsons cross and sent the ball rocketing into the top corner. That was the cue for a minor pitch invasion, followed by the full-scale version when the final whistle blew.

Two young men were particularly pleased. Twenty-year-old Cork commented: 'It was one of the most important goals I have scored. Dario's given me a lot of confidence this season and I see my future with the Club'. Seventeen-year-old Wally Downes was drafted in at the eleventh hour for his first time debut. 'The first I knew that I was playing, was at five o'clock when the manager read out the names on the team sheet,' said the talented youngster. 'I enjoyed every minute of it out there.' Both men would be around long enough to savour First Division football wearing the blue of Wimbledon.

WIMBLEDON: Goddard, Perkins, Eames, Galliers, Bowgett, Cunningham, Leslie, Ketteridge, Downes (Knowles), Cork, Parsons.
YORK CITY: Brown, Kay, Walsh, Pugh, Faulkner, Clements, Ford, Stronach, Wellings (Randall), McDonald, Staniforth.
CROWD: 3,897 REFEREE: Mr A. Grey (Gt Yarmouth)

Ray Knowles side-foots the Dons' first goal past Pompey's Peter Mellor.

ABOVE: That man Knowles again — this time with a diving header to put Wimbledon 2-1 up against Portsmouth. BELOW: The two Alans — Cork of Wimbledon and Ball of Southampton — in a challenge for the ball.

ABOVE: John Leslie (No 7) forces home the equaliser with the York City defence no where. BELOW: Goalscorer Allan Cork fires in a shot as two York defenders look on.

1978 - 79 AT A GLANCE

DATE	OPPONENTS	H/A	Res.	Att.	1	2	3	4	5	6	7	8	9	10	11	12
Aug. 12	Southend (FLC1)	A	0-1	4,845	Goddard	Bryant	Eames	Denny	Galvin	Donaldson	Leslie	Briley	Connell	Cork 1	Summerill	Galliers
15	Southend (FLC1)	H	4-1 *	2,687	Goddard	Bryant	Eames	Galliers 1	Galvin	Donaldson	Leslie	Briley	Denny 1	Cork 1	Summerill	Ketteridge (7)
19	Aldershot	A	1-1	3,510	Goddard	Bryant 1	Eames	Galliers	Galvin	Donaldson	Leslie	Briley	Summerill	Cork 3	Parsons	Ketteridge
22	Port Vale	H	1-0	2,638	Goddard	Bryant	Eames	Galliers	Galvin	Donaldson	Leslie 1	Briley	Connell	Cork	Parsons	Ketteridge
26	Northampton Town	H	4-1	2,644	Goddard	Bryant	Eames	Galliers	Galvin	Donaldson	Leslie	Denny	Connell	Cork	Parsons	Denny (8)
29	Everton (FLC2)	A	0-8	23,137	Goddard	Bryant	Eames	Galliers	Galvin	Donaldson	Leslie	Briley	Connell	Cork	Parsons	Summerill
Sept. 1	Stockport County	A	1-0	5,604	Goddard	Bryant	Eames	Galliers	Galvin	Donaldson	Leslie	Briley	Denny	Cork 1	Parsons	Knowles (7)
9	Wigan Athletic	H	2-1	3,217	Goddard	Bryant	Eames 1	Galliers	Galvin	Donaldson	Leslie	Ketteridge	Denny 1	Cork	Parsons	Knowles (10)
12	Grimsby Town	A	2-2	6,794	Goddard	Bryant 1	Eames	Galliers	Galvin	Donaldson	Leslie	Knowles	Denny	Cork 1	Summerill	Ketteridge
16	Newport County	A	3-1	2,903	Goddard	Bryant	Eames	Galliers	Galvin	Donaldson	Leslie 2	Denny	Knowles	Cork 1	Summerill	Ketteridge
23	Reading	H	1-0	5,011	Goddard	Bryant	Eames	Galliers	Galvin	Donaldson	Leslie	Denny	Knowles	Cork 1	Summerill	Parsons (9)
25	Rochdale	A	0-0	1,263	Goddard	Bryant	Eames	Galliers	Galvin	Donaldson	Leslie	Denny	Knowles	Cork	Summerill	Parsons
30	Bradford	H	2-1	2,819	Goddard	Bryant	Eames	Galliers	Galvin	Donaldson	Leslie	Denny 1	Knowles	Cork	Parsons 1	Ketteridge (7)
Oct. 7	York City	A	4-1	3,329	Goddard	Bryant	Eames	Galliers	Galvin	Donaldson	Leslie 1	Denny	Knowles 1	Cork 1	Parsons 1	Ketteridge
14	Scunthorpe United	H	3-1	3,819	Goddard	Bryant	Eames	Galliers	Galvin	Donaldson	Leslie 2	Denny	Knowles	Cork 1	Parsons	Cowley (7)
17	Crewe Alexandra	H	1-1	3,555	Goddard	Bryant	Eames	Galliers	Galvin	Donaldson	Leslie	Denny	Knowles	Cork 1	Parsons	Cowley (8)
21	Huddersfield Town	A	0-3	3,374	Goddard	Bryant	Eames	Galliers	Galvin	Donaldson	Leslie	Cowley	Knowles	Cork	Parsons	Summerill (9)
28	Doncaster Rovers	H	3-2	3,252	Goddard	Perkins	Eames	Galliers	Bryant	Donaldson	Leslie 2	Haverson	Knowles	Cork 1	Parsons	Summerill (7)
Nov. 4	Barnsley	A	1-3	11,761	Goddard	Bryant	Perkins	Galliers	Galvin 1	Donaldson	Leslie	Haverson	Knowles	Cork	Parsons	Cowley
11	Stockport County	H	2-0	3,177	Goddard	Perkins	Eames	Galliers	Galvin	Donaldson	Leslie	Haverson	Denny 2	Cork	Parsons	Knowles
18	Northampton Town	A	1-1	3,623	Goddard	Perkins	Eames	Galliers	Galvin	Donaldson	Leslie 1	Haverson	Denny	Cork	Parsons	Knowles
25	Gravesend (FAC1)	A	0-0	3,578	Goddard	Perkins	Haverson	Galliers	Galvin	Donaldson	Leslie	Denny	Connell	Cork	Parsons	Briley (9)
28	Gravesend (FAC1 Replay)	H	1-0	3,369	Goddard	Perkins	Haverson	Galliers	Galvin	Donaldson	Leslie	Denny	Connell	Cork 1	Parsons	Briley (9)
Dec. 2	Halifax Town	H	2-1	2,374	Goddard	Perkins	Haverson	Galliers	Galvin	Donaldson	Leslie	Briley	Denny	Cork 2	Parsons	Knowles
9	Hartlepool United	A	1-1	3,098	Goddard	Perkins	Haverson	Galliers	Galvin	Donaldson	Leslie	Briley	Denny 1	Cork	Parsons	Knowles
16	Bournemouth (FAC2)	H	1-1	3,308	Goddard	Bryant	Haverson	Galliers	Galvin	Donaldson	Leslie	Briley	Denny 1	Cork	Parsons	Knowles
23	AFC Bournemouth	A	2-1	3,922	Goddard	Bryant	Haverson	Galliers 1	Galvin	Eames	Leslie	Briley	Denny 1	Cork	Cowley	Knowles (7)
26	Portsmouth	H	2-4	8,084	Goddard	Bryant	Haverson	Galliers	Galvin	Eames	Leslie	Briley	Knowles 2	Cork	Cowley	Driver (7)
28	Bournemouth (FAC2 Replay)	A	2-1	7,192	Goddard	Perkins	Eames	Ketteridge	Galvin	Donaldson	Parsons 1	Briley	Knowles	Cork 1	Haverson	Denny (6)
Jan. 9	Southampton (FAC3)	H	0-2	9,254	Goddard	Perkins	Eames	Ketteridge	Galvin	Denny	Parsons	Briley	Knowles	Cork	Haverson	Leslie (9)
Feb. 3	Rochdale	H	3-2	3,166	Goddard	Bryant	Haverson	Ketteridge	Galvin 1	Perkins	Driver	Briley	Leslie	Denny 1	Parsons 1	Knowles (7)
14	Wigan Athletic	A	2-1	6,704	Goddard	Bryant	Eames	Haverson	Galvin	Perkins	Leslie 2	Ketteridge	Denny	Cork	Parsons	Driver
28	Torquay United	A	6-1	2,739	Priddy	Bryant	Haverson	Ketteridge	Galvin	Perkins	Leslie 1	Galliers	Denny	Cork 4	Parsons	Driver (8)
Mar. 3	Huddersfield Town	H	2-1	3,265	Goddard	Bryant	Haverson	Ketteridge	Galvin	Perkins	Leslie 1	Galliers	Denny	Cork	Parsons	Driver (9)
[illegible]	[illegible]	[illegible]	[illegible]	[illegible]	[illegible]	Bryant	Haverson	Ketteridge	Galvin	Perkins	Leslie	Galliers	Denny	Cork	Parsons	Driver (11)

31	Hereford United	H	2-0	2,636	Goddard	Perkins	Haverson	Briley	Galvin	Cunningham	Leslie 1	Galliers	Knowles	Cork 1	Parsons	Denny (11)
Apr. 4	Bradford City	A	0-1	2,701	Goddard	Perkins	Haverson	Galliers	Galvin	Cunningham	Leslie	Briley	Knowles	Cork	Ketteridge	Denny (7)
7	Halifax Town	A	1-2	1,572	Goddard	Perkins	Haverson	Galliers	Galvin	Cunningham	Denny	Briley	Knowles	Cork	Ketteridge 1	Parsons (7)
10	AFC Bournemouth	H	4-0	3,205	Goddard	Haverson	Donaldson	Galliers	Bowgett	Cunningham	Leslie 1	Briley	Knowles	Cork 2	Parsons 1	Driver (8)
14	Portsmouth	A	0-0	11,453	Goddard	Haverson	Perkins	Galliers	Bowgett	Cunningham	Leslie	Briley	Knowles	Cork	Parsons	Driver (9)
16	Torquay United	H	5-0	4,171	Goddard	Haverson	Perkins	Galliers 1	Bowgett	Cunningham 1	Leslie 1	Briley	Knowles 1	Cork	Parsons 1	Driver
21	Darlington	A	1-1	1,674	Goddard	Haverson	Perkins	Galliers	Bowgett	Cunningham	Leslie 1	Briley	Knowles	Cork	Parsons	Bryant (6)
25	Crewe Alexandra	A	2-1	1,254	Goddard	Haverson	Perkins	Galliers	Bowgett	Cunningham	Leslie 1	Briley	Knowles	Cork	Parsons 1	Bryant (3)
28	Hartlepool United	H	3-1 *	3,540	Goddard	Briley	Haverson	Galliers 1	Bowgett	Cunningham 1	Leslie	Ketteridge	Knowles	Cork	Parsons	Bryant (11)
May 2	Reading	A	0-1	13,131	Goddard	Bryant	Donaldson	Galliers	Bowgett	Cunningham	Leslie	Briley	Knowles	Cork	Parsons	Ketteridge (9)
5	Hereford United	H	0-0	3,809	Goddard	Perkins	Donaldson	Galliers	Bowgett	Cunningham	Leslie	Briley	Ketteridge	Cork	Haverson	Dziadulewicz
8	Scunthorpe United	A	0-2	1,777	Goddard	Perkins	Eames	Galliers	Bowgett	Cunningham	Leslie	Briley	Ketteridge	Cork	Haverson	Dziadulewicz
11	York City	H	2-1	3,897	Goddard	Perkins	Eames	Galliers	Bowgett	Cunningham	Leslie 1	Ketteridge	Downes	Cork 1	Parsons	Knowles (9)
14	Barnsley	H	1-1	5,794	Goddard	Perkins	Eames	Galliers	Bowgett	Cunningham	Leslie	Ketteridge	Downes 1	Cork	Parsons	Knowles (3)
17	Darlington	H	2-0 *	3,638	Goddard	Perkins	Haverson	Galliers	Harwood	Cunningham	Ketteridge	Briley	Dziadulewicz	Cork	Downes	Leslie (5)

* own goal

FINAL TABLE

LEAGUE DIVISION FOUR

	P	W	D	L	F	A	W	D	L	F	A	Pts
Reading	46	19	3	1	49	8	7	10	6	27	27	65
Grimsby Town	46	15	5	3	51	23	11	4	8	31	26	61
WIMBLEDON	46	18	3	2	50	20	7	8	8	28	26	61
Barnsley	46	15	5	3	47	23	9	8	6	26	19	61
Aldershot	46	16	5	2	38	14	4	12	7	25	33	57
Wigan Athletic	46	14	5	4	40	24	7	8	8	23	24	55
Portsmouth	46	13	7	3	35	12	7	5	11	27	36	52
Newport City	46	12	5	6	39	28	9	5	9	27	27	52
Huddersfield Town	46	13	8	2	32	15	5	3	15	25	38	47
York City	46	11	6	6	33	24	7	5	11	18	31	47
Torquay United	46	14	4	5	38	24	5	4	14	20	41	46
Scunthorpe United	46	12	3	8	33	30	5	8	10	21	30	45
Hartlepool United	46	7	12	4	35	28	6	6	11	22	38	44
Hereford United	46	12	8	3	35	18	3	5	15	18	35	43
Bradford City	46	11	5	7	38	26	6	4	13	24	42	43
Port Vale	46	8	10	5	29	28	6	4	13	28	42	42
Stockport County	46	11	5	7	33	21	3	7	13	25	39	40
Bournemouth	46	11	6	6	34	19	3	5	15	13	29	39
Northampton Town	46	12	4	7	40	30	3	5	15	24	46	39
Rochdale	46	11	4	8	25	26	4	5	14	22	38	39
Darlington	46	8	8	7	25	21	3	7	13	24	45	37
Doncaster R.	46	8	8	7	25	22	5	3	15	25	51	37
Halifax Town	46	7	5	11	24	32	2	3	18	15	40	26
Crewe Alexandra	46	3	7	13	24	41	3	7	13	19	49	26

GOALS AND GAMES

APPEARANCES AND GOALSCORERS

	Appearances			Goals	
	Lge	Cup	Sub	Lge	Cup
Paul Bowgett	11				
Les Briley	26	5			
Jeff Bryant	27	4	3	2	
Roger Connell	2	4			
Alan Cork	45	8		22	3
Fran Cowley	3		3		
Tommy Cunningham	15			3	
Paul Denny	24	7	4	7	2
Dave Donaldson	23	7			
Wally Downes	3		1		
Phil Driver	3		7	1	1
Mark Dziadulewicz	1		1		
Terry Eames	26	5		1	
Steve Galliers	44	5		3	1
Dave Galvin	33	8		2	
Ray Goddard	45	8			
Lee Harwood	1				
Paul Haverson	26	5	1	1	
Steve Ketteridge	15	2	2	2	
Ray Knowles	23	2	8	5	
John Leslie	44	6	1	19	
Steve Parsons	34	6	3		
Steve Perkins	26	4			
Paul Priddy	1				
Phil Summerill	5	2	2		

Wimbledon FC 1978-79. Back row: Steve Ketteridge, Alan Cork, Steve Parsons, Ray Goddard, Roger Connell, Dave Galvin, Phil Summerill. Front row: Brian Bithell, Steve Galliers, Les Briley, John Leslie, Terry Eames and Paul Denny.

ABOVE: Steve Parsons (centre) receives the congratulations of Steve Ketteridge (No. 7) after scoring a spectacular goal in the League Cup-tie with Aldershot. BELOW: Wally Downes applies the touch to score the Dons' first goal against Orient at Plough Lane. Billy Jennings and Mervyn Day can only admire his acrobatics.

Inexperience and Relegation 1979-80

A solid start

During the summer of 1979 the Club held its annual dinner, attended by over 200 people, at the Dog and Fox in Wimbledon Village. To commemorate promotion to the Third Division, stainless steel plaques were presented to the players, directors and management staff who served the Club during the 1978-79 season.

Tribute was also paid to former manager Allen Batsford and his former assistant, Brian Hall, who both attended the dinner, for their achievement in winning the three Southern League titles that gave Wimbledon the platform to enter the Football League.

In his speech Ron Noades confirmed that Wimbledon would be staying at Plough Lane. 'We've got no intention of moving but the pre-emption clause means our borrowing power is totally out of line with the value of the facilities we have got.' When the Club purchased the freehold in the 1940s, the value of the ground was set at £8,000, with the agreement that, if football was no longer played there, the Council could buy it back at the same price.

Noades continued: 'We are not asking the council for any money, just to raise the pre-emption value to the sort of level where we borrow without Club officials putting up their own money as security'. It was also announced that evening that Bernie Coleman, the Club's President since 1972, would be taking a seat on the board, and that he would be replaced as President by Wimbledon MP and Attorney General, Sir Michael Havers.

As pre-season training began in July, manager Gradi was stressing the need for quality. 'I have ordered a change in our style — and the aim is to improve the quality of football at Plough Lane. I want the passing to improve and the control too.' He also planned sweeping tactical changes in the defence — having three defenders marking man for man and the fourth as a sweeper. He described the wobble that affected Wimbledon towards the end of last season as a possible blessing in disguise. 'I am hoping that the attack of nerves near the end works in our favour next time. It was an important period for my young team and the good point is that they battled through.'

Gradi was also active in the transfer market, bringing in forward Mark Dziadulewicz from Southend for £3,000 and midfielder Craig Richards on a free transfer, and three defenders, Lee Harwood, £2,500 from Southampton, Steve Jones, £13,500 from Walsall, and Peter Brown on a free from Chelsea. There were departures too — stalwarts Dave Galvin, Jeff Bryant, Roger Connell and Dave Donaldson all left as Gradi put his faith unashamedly in youth.

The new players and tactical systems were all tried out during four pre-season games. First Division Chelsea were beaten 2-1 on 28 July before a two-match West Country tour in early August. First Dawlish and then Yeovil held the Dons, 1-1 and 0-0 respectively. The final match before the season proper involved a home game with local rivals Crystal Palace, which was lost 1-0 due to a Steve Perkins own goal.

For the third season in a row, Wimbledon easily won their two-leg League Cup-tie. In the first leg at Plough Lane the Dons outclassed Aldershot 4-1 with the entire attack — Parsons, Cork, Leslie and Knowles — scoring. More goals from Leslie and Knowles led to a first ever win at the Recreation Ground in the 2nd leg.

The historic first match in the Third Division took place on 11 August 1979 and proved a tough baptism. A 3-2 defeat at home to Chester was down to defensive errors. Two down in 35 minutes, John Leslie pulled a goal back with a header. Welsh International Ian Edwards made it 3-1 on the hour and Alan Cork's goal with five minutes left was no more than a consolation for most of the 3,549 crowd.

Their first 3rd Division points came in a midweek win at Exeter. Man-of-the-match Steve Parsons scored the first after 74 minutes with a dipping volley and John Leslie wrapped it up seven minutes later. However, the celebrations were short-lived as the following Saturday visitors Southend left Plough Lane with both points; one goal from Colin Morris did the damage.

The League Cup 2nd Round had now been turned into a two-leg format. Wimbledon had drawn 2nd Division Orient and dominated the first hour of the first leg at Brisbane Road. Two up with goals from Parsons and Leslie, the Dons eased up and the home side roared back to snatch a scarely deserved draw. This was followed by the first of many trips to famous old clubs, which saw the Dons well beaten at Blackpool by three goals to nil.

The second leg of the League Cup-tie proved to be a real nail-biter. Wimbledon took the lead through Downes in the first half but a second half equaliser meant it was 1-1 at full time. With two minutes of extra time left, Parsons scored a spectacular goal, but a lapse of concentration led to John Margerrison equalising seconds later. It meant a penalty shoot-out and, with tension mounting, both sides held their nerve as the score reached 4-4. Up stepped big Joe Mayo and Ray Goddard turned his shot to safety *via* a post. It was goalkeeper Goddard himself who took the decisive kick, thundering the winner past Mervyn Day.

The first home win in the Third Division was not long in arriving. Still on a high from the League Cup win, they beat Blackburn 1-0 with a Ray Knowles header. Two wins from five matches and in the 3rd Round of the League Cup; it was a pleasing start. It was to get so much harder.

Wally Downes is beaten to this header in the second half of the match with Blackburn Rovers.

Gradi signs up

The long-term confidence felt by the Club in its management team was shown as they signed five year contracts. Manager Dario Gradi's contract of around £100,000 over five years made him one of the highest earners outside the 1st Division. His assistant Dave Bassett and the youth team coach Alan Gillett also signed five year terms. 'We are still in the process of building the Club,' commented Noades. 'Our aim is to get everything right over a long period and that involves the Stadium, the team and the youth set-up.'

Back on the field things were proving less easy to plan for. The first of two visits to Plymouth in ten days brought no reward. Dave Kemp, on his debut for Argyle, scored twice in a 3-0 defeat for the Dons. Only a superb show from Ray Goddard kept the score respectable in the next game at Gillingham. A string of fine saves included a penalty stop, but he was finally beaten by a deflected shot.

Dario Gradi's frustration boiled over at home to Brentford. 'I threatened some of the players with the sack at half-time,' he fumed. 'They played much better after that.' Brentford dominated the opening half but Wimbledon battled hard in the second half to force a 0-0 draw. But Steve Jones' sending off added to the gloom as the Dons sank to the bottom of the table for the first time.

A lack of experience was beginning to tell, with only goalkeeper Ray Goddard aged over 25. His regular defence featured Steve Perkins and Steve Jones at full back and Paul Bowgett and Tommy Cunningham in the centre. Three more Steves patrolled the midfield — Galliers, Ketteridge and Parsons — while up front John Leslie, Alan Cork and Ray Knowles were normally on view.

A lack of goals was the main problem with only five in eight Leagues games so far. Returning to Home Park for a League Cup 3rd Round tie, the Dons found themselves with their backs to the wall against a confident Plymouth side. The defensive tactics were successful, as a 0-0 draw ensured a replay in London.

Before that game Wimbledon had travelled to Bury in the battle for League points. The debut of former Chelsea midfield man, Ray Lewington, was a boost for the team and the 2-1 win lifted them off the bottom. On loan from Vancouver Whitecaps, Lewington was a major influence on the game. 'He's what Alan Ball is to Southampton,' enthused Gradi. 'He's a natural leader. He'll control and calm players down.'

The return with Plymouth was another hard-fought affair. Neither side was able to penetrate well-organised defences for much of the night and it was goal-less again at full time. With under ten minutes of extra time remaining, leading scorer John Leslie broke the deadlock to put the Dons in the 4th Round for the first time.

The long haul to Carlisle produced a point but Gradi blasted the team. 'The worst performance of the season. At least our goalkeeper had a marvellous game.' Ahead in nine minutes the Dons only seemed interested in survival. A 31st minute equaliser meant a long second-half siege which they rarely lifted.

Despite that, Wimbledon extended their unbeaten run to seven games, with three points from home games against Exeter and Swindon. One minute into the second half of the Exeter game and the Dons were 2-0 down, but a battling fight back ensured a point. It might have been two, but Alan Cork's shot hit the net a fraction of a second after the full-time whistle. It was a Cork double which saw off Swindon in a fine team performance that lifted the Club to eighteenth place. It was a false dawn; it was two and a half months before another League win was recorded.

ABOVE: Brentford defender Paul Shrubb takes evasive action as Steve Galliers powers his shot goalwards. BELOW: Ray Lewington, on his home debut, arrives too late to stop this clearance by Brian Bason of Plymouth in the League Cup repay.

Winter gloom

As winter approached there were hopes of a steady rise up the table. These increased as a dour, defensive performance ensured a 0-0 draw at Chesterfield and the Dons made it eight games unbeaten. But the run came to a sudden halt in Essex the following Tuesday. Badly hit by injuries — Terry Eames was recalled and Mark Dziadulewicz made his full debut — Wimbledon were no match for a rampant Colchester side, who rammed home four goals without reply.

Two glamorous home games followed. First, once mighty Sheffield Wednesday starred in a seven goal thriller, winning 4-3. Gradi fumed that his players had been overawed by playing against such a famous team. Worse was to follow as Swindon Town knocked the Dons out of the League Cup. Steve Perkins equalised Swindon's 53rd minute opener, only for Chic Bates to score a simple winner with six minutes left. The large Wiltshire contingent in the 7,400 crowd went home happy.

Wimbledon dropped into twenty-first place after a 3-1 defeat at Chester. After only four minutes, home defender Walker lobbed his own 'keeper, to give the Dons a dream start, but three second-half goals ended their hopes. The first was scored by a promising young eighteen-year-old striker — Ian Rush.

Wimbledon were winning praise rather than points. For example, Colchester manager Bobby Roberts commented after their 4-0 win that: 'they are still the best team we have played at home all season'. A succession of opposing managers lauded the team but took the points. What a contrast to later years, when the Dons would be criticised for their style of play as they won matches but not hearts.

Ironically it was Colchester who were the next visitors in the return League match. The U's — in third place — were quickly 2-0 down through a Steve Parsons free kick and penalty. They rallied to force a 3-3 draw. Two 1-0 defeats followed, at home to Rotherham in front of only 2,700 and then at Grimsby. Once again the Dons were rooted to the bottom of the table.

Ten goal John Leslie rocked the Club with a transfer request before the FA Cup trip to Gillingham. Gradi played down speculation, saying: 'I don't anticipate selling any player currently in the team. I only want to strengthen it'. Ironically, Leslie dislocated a shoulder after 17 minutes at the Priestfield Stadium and missed most of a solid display which earned a replay.

He was fit enough to star with a two-goal display in a 4-2 replay win. Mark Dziadulewicz scored the most spectacular goal of the evening when his 20-yard chip dipped over goalkeeper Hillyard. Leslie still had severe brusing left over from the first match but wanted to play. 'He did a good job for us,' commented Gradi, 'but he still wants to leave. I want to sell him if he wants to go and I want a replacement as soon as possible'.

It was Alan Cork, without a goal since October, who saved the day with an equaliser two minutes from time at Hull on the first day of December. Meanwhile a Dons Youth Team, including Kevin Gage, Mark Morris, Glyn Hodges and Paul Fishenden, were through to the Youth Cup Third Round, beating Fulham 3-1.

It was top *v* bottom as Sheffield United came to Plough Lane a week later and left with a 1-1 draw. Said boss Gradi: 'The game was of such a high standard that it was very difficult for me to stop enthusing about it at half time instead of talking about how we were getting on'. High standard or not, the Dons were still bottom.

Bad weather curtailed the League action for three weeks, but the visit of 4th Division leaders Portsmouth for an FA Cup 2nd Round tie attracted a 10,000+ crowd. Although Pompey were the country's leading scorers, there were no goals in a tense affair. The replay took place at Fratton Park on Christmas Eve and, after trailing 2-0 after 25 minutes, the Dons roared back for a 3-3 draw, with recalled striker Paul Denny on target twice. It was so exciting that, when it was announced that the last ferry to the Isle of Wight was about to leave, no-one moved.

The final game of 1978 saw Paul Denny make it four goals in two games as Wimbledon won the relegation clash at Southend 3-1. It was the first League success in ten attempts. A year that had begun with Wimbledon leading Division 4 ended with them bottom of Division 3.

A toss of a coin brought Portsmouth back to Plough Lane for the 2nd replay of the FA Cup-tie. Youngsters Wally Downes and Mark Dziadulewicz were both dropped and defenders Tommy Cunningham and Steve Perkins recalled. The changes made no difference, as a 13th minute Jeff Hemmerman goal dumped the disappointing Dons out of the Cup.

Gradi still managed to hit an optimistic note: 'We have been playing well enough over the last few weeks. We've still got half way to go and I'm sure that if we maintain our form we'll get out of trouble. Just because we went out of the Cup and we're bottom doesn't mean there's a crisis. If we have got a problem then it is our record of inconsistency. We are becoming more consistent but we must improve further'.

Brave words but, with only 2,688 in attendace, Wimbledon lost their first League match of the 1980s 2-1 at home to Blackpool. Nineteen-year-old goalkeeper Dave Beasant made his debut in place of the injured Goddard. It was a game he will want to forget. With the score at 1-1 and only six minutes left, a Morris cross shot slipped first through his arms, then through his legs and in at the far post. He did not appear again that season but returned to become one of the lynchpins of the Dons' rise to prominence in the years to come.

Three tough away trips followed: first a heavy defeat at Blackburn, then a controversial 1-1 draw at Mansfield, where Ray Goddard was sent off in the tunnel for disputing the late equaliser, and finally a victory at Brentford. The star at Griffin Park was Steve Parsons, whose 18-yard shot in the 27th minute proved the only goal.

Two wins in successive home games lifted morale and raised hopes of avoiding relegation. Mick Smith, a £12,500 signing from Lincoln City, made his home debut against Gillingham. He was part of a solid defensive display which shut out the Gills. At the other end it was transfer-listed Leslie who secured both points with a header from a corner. Six days later, Plymouth were beaten at Plough Lane for the second time that season, as John Leslie took his tally to fifteen, with a goal in each half securing a 3-1 win.

Now two off the bottom and with games in hand over all the other clubs, Wimbledon looked to be hitting form at the right time. Sadly they managed to win only two of the remaining eighteen games.

Although beaten at Swindon in their next trip, they could count themselves unlucky after dominating for long spells. The visit of Bury provided an unusual experience — playing a side below them in the table. A pitiful display led to a 1-0 defeat as the low crowds began to cause problems financially. Chairman Ron Noades needed to raise some money to balance the books and this led to two key players leaving Plough Lane.

Unconnected with finances, Ray Lewington played his last game in a 1-1 draw with Chesterfield. After 30 consecutive appearances his loan spell ended and he returned to Canada's Vancouver Whitecaps. A 3-0 defeat at Reading followed before Steve Parsons made his final appearance in a Dons shirt at Hillsborough, after which he transferred to Orient for £45,000. The 3-1 defeat at the hands of promotion-chasing Sheffield Wednesday was seen by over 20,000 — the largest crowd to watch Wimbledon play that season.

As the Dons moved into the dreaded bottom spot again, Les Briley signed for Aldershot, his last game being in the 2-1 home defeat by Barnsley. Gradi maintained a positive front: 'I was sorry to see Les go but it's a god move for him. I didn't want to lose Les but Aldershot came in for him with a good offer'.

LEFT: Steve Parsons harasses Chesterfield's Shaun O'Neil into conceding a throw-in. RIGHT: Paul Bowgett clears from a young Ian Rush at Sealand Road, Chester. BELOW: Steve Galliers rides the challenge of Rotherham's Mark Rhodes.

LEFT: Steve Parsons is crowded out by two identikit Gillingham defenders in the FA Cup-tie at Priestfield Stadium. RIGHT: Pat Kruse fails to block the shot as Steve Parsons scores the only goal at Brentford. BELOW: Roy Carter and Alan Cork are beaten by the pace of the through ball at Swindon's County Ground.

The relegation trap-door

By mid-March, Wimbledon fans knew in their hearts that relegation was inevitable. The prospects of staying in the Third Division were made worse by Neil Cooper's last minute winner in the home game with Barnsley. No-one was prepared to admit defeat — with Dons boss Dario Gradi declaring: 'There's a long way to go yet' — but Wimbledon needed to reach 40 points to have a chance of survival. That looked a long way off with 15 more points needed from 12 games.

The sales of Parsons and Briley, together with Lewington's departure, weakened the team at a crucial time. In return only full back Gary Armstrong joined the Dons — from Gillingham for £15,000. Where did the profit go? Chairman Noades explained that the money went on 'the purchase of Armstrong, to the ground improvements scheme and towards the Club's financial deficit from last year'.

'Dario's brief is to make money from the team without weakening its strength. Until the ground is of a standard suitable for the Second Division, he will always be expected to make us money,' continued Noades. 'This comes down to good housekeeping, Parsons was £100 from Walton, he went for £42,000. Briley was £16,000, he went for £40,000.'

Without the departed men, Wimbledon stuttered to a 0-0 draw against a disappointing Carlisle side in their next game. A poor Friday night crowd of 2,093 saw the Dons create plenty of chances but fail to find the net. John Leslie was denied a second-half hat-trick by the Carlisle 'keeper Swinburne, while at the other end Peter Beardsley's 65th minute drive was well turned round by Goddard.

There were debuts for Gary Armstrong and loan-signing Brian Klug at Oxford. It was an evening of defensive errors in the Dons rearguard as the home side swept to a 4-1 win. 'On that performance Fourth Division football is about all we deserve,' fumed Gradi. It left Wimbledon bottom with 26 points and only 10 games left.

A drab 0-0 draw at Rotherham's Millmoor ground was followed by the visit of top-of-the-table Grimsby Town. Having gone 1-0 up through Paul Denny's header, the Dons found themselves 6-1 down within 20 minutes of the second half. Despite fighting back they ended up beaten 6-3.

Former Millwall goalkeeper Ray Goddard received a warm reception from all sides of the ground as he returned to the Den with the Dons on Easter Saturday. An exciting game on a hard and bumpy pitch saw the teams having to settle for a point each at the end of a 2-2 draw. Alan Cork's first goal of 1980 ensured the point in the 75th minute.

Paul Bowgett received the Easter card no-one wanted — a red one in Wimbledon's 1-1 draw with Reading at Plough Lane on Easter Monday. He was sent off for an 80th minute head butt on Pat Earles. Eight minutes earlier Steve Ketteridge had volleyed the Dons ahead, with Wayne Wanklyn equalising two minutes later.

Following a 4-0 defeat at Barnsley and a 3-1 home reverse against Oxford, manager Dario Gradi accepted that relegation was inevitable. 'I accept the fact that we're not staying up,' he said. 'I can't see who there is we can beat. We will keep fighting, keep on trying to play. But we can't win those little individual battles; we're not strong enough, we're just boys.'

The next morning a Press Association announcement was telexed to all the media, announcing that every one of the players was up for sale. While this was an exaggeration, Gradi had been told by Noades to raise an additional £40,000 by selling players. What followed was a public relations disaster.

Many papers ran the story, implying that all the players would be sold. An article in *The Sunday Times* particularly angered Chairman Noades, who called it 'a disgrace to journalism'. The *Nationwide* programme on television ran a piece, showing a rift between Chairman and manager.

The Club was inexperienced in handling the national media and the Chairman and the manager were interviewed in different places and at different times without being aware of the programme content. Players were also interviewed without being briefed by the Club on the true position. Gradi attempted to explain: 'The names of all the players were circulated to the Clubs, inviting offers. That doesn't mean I'm going to sell everybody. Then if I get offers, say, for six of them, I can accept the best. The money is necessary to rebuild'.

It was to the credit of the players that they responded by taking five points from the final four games. First, Hull City were beaten 3-2 with two goals from John Leslie and a Wally Downes penalty. Then Downes scored again with Alan Cork also on target in a 2-2 draw with Millwall.

Another penalty from Wally Downes — this one in the 81st minute — appeared to have earned the Dons a draw at Sheffield United, but Pedro Verde's shot squirmed under Goddard for the winner with only four minutes remaining. The final match of the season saw Wimbledon 3-0 up within 46 minutes against Mansfield. Goals from Player of the Year Steve Galliers, Tommy Cunningham and Alan Cork left them coasting, but Mansfield hit back to end only 3-2 down. It was all to no avail as the Dons finished bottom and returned to the delights of Division Four.

End of season friendlies restored some pride. Fulham were beaten 2-0 in the West London Cup and Tooting defeated 3-1 in the Lanes Cup. Chairman Ron Noades remained defiant about the future. 'We will be pushing next year for a return to the Third Division,' he said. 'We will be better next time for the experience of this season. Relegation is just a hiccough in the Club's growth. It's nothing more than that.'

In a reference to recent publicity suggesting the whole first team was up for sale, Mr Noades said there would be few changes to the playing staff in 1980-81. 'This is just a load of hot air about nothing,' he said. 'We are in a stronger financial position at this moment than we have been for the last three years.'

'It's ludicrous to suggest that we want to sell all our players. If we receive a fee for a player, it might not be enough. And if we sold him, we might not be able replace him.' But he added: 'We are prepared to sell one or two if someone tempts us with the right offer'.

ABOVE: John Leslie volleys over during the 1-1 home draw with Reading. BELOW: Millwall 'keeper, John Jackson, gathers safely despite the efforts of the onrushing Brian Klug.

LEFT: Chester's David Lloyd takes the ball off Alan Cork's head. RIGHT: John Leslie volleys over in the first half against Chester. BELOW: John Leslie salutes Steve Perkins who has just supplied the cross for the Wimbledon goal. RIGHT: Alan Cork makes the score 3-4 with just minutes of the game remaining.

Memorable Matches 1979-80

18 August 1979: FOOTBALL LEAGUE DIVISION THREE

Wimbledon 2 *Leslie, Cork*

Chester 3 *Ruggiero, Henderson, Edwards*

Wimbledon paid the full price for a series of missed chances and defensive errots in their first-ever match in Division Three. Manager Dario Gradi had introduced a new sweeper system during pre-season matches which was intended to stem the flow of goals. There were clearly lessons still to be learned as the Dons lost a match they should have won.

Chester, player-managed by 36-year-old former Manchester City man Alan Oakes, were gifted a two goal lead and their fortunes held as the home side contrived to miss a host of worthwhile chances.

'We might have been beaten,' said Gradi, 'but there is no sour taste. As long as we keep creating chances the wins will come but our mistakes cost us dear. If we can keep playing well as a team we shall win more games than we lose.'

'If we had not looked like scoring I would be worried,' he continued. 'I never felt the game was lost and if we played Chester ten times down here I would take us to win nine times out of ten.'

Chester took the lead in fortuitous style in the 34th minute. Peter Henderson looked offside when Oakes' pass found him on the left. His cross was knocked straight into the path of John Ruggiero, who made no mistake. Within sixty seconds it was two — Oakes sending Henderson through again down the middle and the pacy winger ran clear to fire past Goddard from 20 yards.

John Leslie made up for his earlier misses when he nipped in to meet Les Briley's corner with a firm header after 40 minutes to leave the half-time score at 2-1.

Welsh International Ian Edwards scored the goal of the game within 10 minutes of the restart. His glorious drive, from twenty yards, should have buried Wimbledon, but they battled back bravely.

The Chester goal appeared to have a charmed life from then on. First Ray Knowles volleyed over from three yards, then Cork missed two free headers. Visiting 'keeper Brian Lloyds somehow denied the Dons in an amazing series of chances which fell to Steve Ketteridge, Cork and finally Steve Parsons.

Alan Cork did pull one goal back with a header in the 85th minute, which ensured a frantic late finale. Paul Bowgett and substitute Steve Galliers both fired shots just wide, but somehow Chester held out.

A relieved Alan Oakes emerged afterwards to praise the battling Dons. 'They will take a lot of stopping if they keep playing like that,' he said. 'Wimbledon just need to sharpen up and then they are going to beat a lot of sides.'

Certainly the Dons remained full of confidence. Striker Alan Cork reflected on the months ahead: 'I'm looking forward to playing in the Third Division,' he said. 'The Fourth was very physical and I got a lot of stick. I expect to be tightly marked again but they will probably let me play a bit more football.' Sadly such optimism looked misplaced as the side began to struggle.

WIMBLEDON: Goddard, Perkins, Jones (Galliers), Briley, Bowgett, Cunningham, Ketteridge, Parsons, Leslie, Cork, Knowles.

CHESTER: Lloyd, Raynor, Walker, Storton, Cottam, Oakes, Jefferies, Ruggiero, Edwards, Henderson, Phillips.

CROWD: 3,549 REFEREE: Mr A. Grey (Gt Yarmouth)

27 October 1979: FOOTBALL LEAGUE DIVISION THREE

Wimbledon 3 *Lesle, Parsons, Cork*

Sheffield Wednesday 4 *Lowey, Curran 2, Smith (pen)*

The visit of this famous old club to Plough Lane produced a seven goal thriller. However, it was the Yorkshire side who went home happy, as another four goals found their way behind a suspect Dons defence which had conceded four at Colchester earlier in the week.

Dons boss Gradi felt the very name 'Sheffield Wednesday' had cost his side success. 'It took the players a whole game to realise that Wednesday were not better than them,' he said. 'They are a name in football. Perhaps we expected more from them, but they did not create many problems. We made the mistakes and defeat was our own fault. How can you score three at home and still lose?'

John Lowey headed Wednesday ahead in the sixth minute after Steve Perkins had allowed Roger Wylde to get in a cross from the left. But Wimbledon hit back with a fine move in the thirteenth minute. A good build-up led to Perkins crossing, Tommy Cunningham flicking on and John Leslie firing home with a close-range scissors kick.

Cheered on by the massed ranks of their supporters, chanting endlessly about their Boxing Day clash with neighbours United, Wednesday took the lead again. A Curran cross flew straight in after 34 minutes with no-one else getting a touch.

An Alan Cork effort was ruled out for offside before the break but, thirteen minutes after the restart, the Dons were gifted an equaliser. Steve Parsons scored after a mistake in the Sheffield defence.

With the match delicately poised, Wimbledon won a free kick on the edge of the box in the 67th minute. Substitute Mark Dziadulewicz's free kick bent over the wall and bounced down off the bar, Terry Curran cleared upfield and Jeff King burst into the Dons penalty area. King was sent flying by goalkeeper Ray Goddard and Mark Smith stepped up to convert the penalty. Those decisive 60 seconds changed the match.

Curran's best was yet to come as his 74th minute dribble caused panic in the Wimbledon defence and he beat Goddard with a low drive. Wednesday's fourth was followed by an audacious piece of quick thinking by Steve Parsons. As Cork kicked off again, Parsons saw Brian Cox off his line in the Sheffield goal. His chip was dipping into the net until a relieved goalkeeper back-pedalled to push the ball over the bar.

With only minutes remaining, Alan Cork scored an easy third after Tommy Cunningham had beaten Cox in the air. It was to no avail and the defeat left Wimbledon fourth from bottom with twelve points from fifteen matches. Wednesday, meanwhile, marched on. By May they were back in the 2nd Division.

Captain Cunningham commented: 'It's the first time I've been in a side which conceded eight goals in two matches. But it was a combination of our mistakes and bad luck'. His manager Gradi agreed: 'We have got to stop making silly mistakes in defence if we are to survive in Division Three. The players have shown that they can do well at this level but we must be more consistent'.

WIMBLEDON: Goddard, Perkins, Jones, Galliers, Bowgett, Cunningham, Ketteridge (Dziadulewicz), Parsons, Leslie, Cork, Lewington.

SHEFFIELD WEDNESDAY: Cox, Johnson, Grant, Mullen, Smith, Leman, Wylde, Porterfield, Lowey, King, Curran.

CROWD: 6,009 REFEREE: Mr J. Sewell (Leics)

29 December 1979: FOOTBALL LEAGUE DIVISION THREE

Soutend United 1 *Polycarpou*
Wimbledon 3 *Denny 2, Cork*

A decade which had started with the Dons in the Southern League managed by Les Henley ended with the side bottom of the Football League Division 3. For the first four years of the 1970s Wimbledon were in the wilderness, their fortunes steadily declining. After Allen Batsford's three years at the helm, the promised land of the Football League had been reached. Now Dario Gradi's side had raced into Division Three, only to find the going tough. The ride remained bumpy for several more years before further giant leaps forward were possible.

This match, against fellow strugglers Southend, proved to be a triumph for the Dons and in particular Paul Denny. He returned to Roots Hall, to the Club that gave him a free transfer three years ealier, to grab two goals that gave the side hope that they would have a happy new year.

With two goals in two games since replacing injured John Leslie, 22-year-old Denny was a man on form. With Leslie fit enough to be on the substitute's bench, it was a timely reminder to his manager of his goal-scoring prowess.

Southend took the lead after just 17 minutes when Andy Polycarpou headed past Ray Goddard. But Wimbledon enjoyed far more possession and were unfortunate to approach the half-time break still one goal behind.

Soon after the restart Steve Galliers pounced on a bad backpass from Dave Cusack, rode a strong challenge, before crossing for Denny to score a simple equaliser.

In the 58th minute another former Southend man, Mark Dziadulewicz, sent over a perfect cross for on-form Alan Cork to drive the ball past Mervyn Cawston. And 15 minutes later the points were secure when the Southend defence failed to clear an inswinging Steve Parsons corner and Denny was on hand to drive the ball home.

The win left Wimbledon unbeaten in seven matches and confident that they would move up the table in 1980. 'We are playing the best football since I have been at Plough Lane and we need to keep our run going,' said Gradi. 'The Division is very tight and it is only because we've dropped silly points that we are bottom.

'We have been playing well enough over the last few weeks,' continued Gradi. 'We've still got half way to go and I'm sure that if we maintain our form we'll get out of trouble. If we have got a problem then it is a record of consistency. We are becoming more consistent, but we must improve on that.' But Wimbledon could not maintain their form, and finished the season bottom of Division Three.

It is interesting to reflect on how one's perspective changes. Viewed from 1970, the chance of a Division Three win at Southend would have seemed a dream. By 1990 however, the aspirations of Wimbledon supporters had changed and concerned Manchester United rather than Southend United. As 1980 started, this match simply seemed to herald the start of a sustained push up the table. It was not to be!

SOUTHEND: Cawston, Moody, Yates, Gray, Cusack, Hadley, Polycarpou, Pountney, Parker, Otulakowski, Nelson; sub: Dudley.

WIMBLEDON: Goddard, Briley, Jones, Galliers, Bowgett, Downes, Dziadulewicz (Leslie), Parsons, Denny, Cork, Lewington.

CROWD: 3,952 REFEREE: Mr M. Taylor (Kent)

29 March 1980: FOOTBALL LEAGUE DIVISION THREE
Wimbledon 3 *Denny, Leslie, Cunningham*
Grimsby Town 6 *Kilmore 3, Drinkell, Mitchell, Cumming*

These two sides had been promoted together the previous May so their respective positions, at the top and bottom of the table, were hard for home fans to take. Chairman Ron Noades wrote in the match programme that 'it portrays the harsh realities of football economics and is an indication of the mammoth problems we will have to overcome if we wish to continue to progress with our ambition to exist in higher divisions'.

The recent sales of Les Briley and Steve Parsons, for which he had been criticised, were forced on the Club by low crowds and poor facilities. Only by improving facilities which would then generate extra cash, he concluded, would Wimbledon be able to achieve what Grimsby were about to do — win promotion in successive years.

The Mariners showed why they were top in an amazing five goal burst in the 20 minutes after half time. The match was only played because Wimbledon officials spent the morning covering the pitch with blankets to soak up the rain. They must have wished they hadn't bothered when they saw a Dons defence unable to soak up pressure.

'Ray Goddard was our best player,' said Gradi. 'The mistakes came from those in front of him. My players just don't seem to be able to learn.'

The last thing Gradi and Goddard told the team as they left the dressing room was that back passes were out. 'The ball is going to stick in the mud, we said,' smouldered the Wimbledon manager; 'So what happens? We go out and start passing back'.

Wimbledon survived one such reckless attempt from Mick Smith after only four minutes. Kevin Kilmore rounded Goddard but Wally Downes was back to clear. In the 26th minute Tommy Cunningham had his manager pulling out his hair in frustration again — and this time Kilmore made no mistake. He waltzed round Goddard to cancel out Paul Denny's 22nd minute header, that had given Wimbledon the lead.

Grimsby boss George Keer was equally critical of his side's first half performance, pointing out to them that they had 'forgotten the basics'. The point went home and within 20 minutes of the restart the promotion-chasing Mariners were 6-1 up.

Kilmore completed the easiest of hat-tricks, and Kevin Drinkell, Bob Mitchel and leading scorer Bob Cumming tucked away the others. All the goals came from simple crosses into the box, which the Wimbledon defence was simply unable to handle.

Both sides made 69th minute substitutions — Phil Driver getting his first game of the season — and within seconds John Leslie had restored some pride, forcing home Mark Dziadulewicz's corner. Cunningham made some amends for his earlier lapse heading home a Steve Ketteridge free-kick, and there the scoring finished.

It was not the end of the chances. Grimsby's Clive Wigginton headed against the bar and Goddard twice spread himself to keep out shots. He also produced a magnificent double save — blocking Mike Brolly's effort, then slithering to his knees to hang on to Joe Waters' header as the midfielder flung himself at the rebound.

Grimsby 'keeper Nigel Batch was in equally sound mood — getting back to tip over a vicious drive from Leslie and blocking a Dziadulewicz blockbuster.

WIMBLEDON: Goddard, Downes, Armstrong, Klug, Smith, Cunningham, Ketteridge, Dziadulewicz, Leslie, Cork, Denny (Driver).

GRIMSBY: Batch, D. Moore, Cumming, Waters, Wigginton, Crombie, Brolly, Kilmore, Drinkell, Mitchel (Crosby), Ford.

CROWD: 2,485 REFEREE: Mr J. Martin (Hants)

LEFT: Steve Galliers challenges Southend's Dave Cusack for the ball. Galliers won the challenge and crossed for Paul Denny to fire home the Dons' first goal. RIGHT: Paul Denny (No 11) puts Wimbledon ahead in the first half against Grimsby. BELOW: Tommy Cunningham makes the score-line more respectable with the Dons third.

1979 - 80 AT A GLANCE

DATE	OPPONENTS	H/A	Res.	Att.	1	2	3	4	5	6	7	8	9	10	11	12
Aug. 11	Aldershot (FLC1:1)	H	4-1	3,508	Goddard	Perkins	Jones	Briley	Bowgett	Cunningham	Ketteridge	Parsons 1	Leslie 1	Cork 1	Knowles 1	Galliers (11)
14	Aldershot (FLC1:2)	A	2-1	3,280	Goddard	Perkins	Jones	Briley	Bowgett	Cunningham	Ketteridge	Parsons	Leslie 1	Cork	Knowles 1	Downes
18	Chester	H	2-3	3,549	Goddard	Perkins	Jones	Briley	Bowgett	Cunningham	Ketteridge	Parsons	Leslie 1	Cork 1	Knowles	Galliers (3)
22	Exeter City	A	2-0	4,051	Goddard	Perkins	Jones	Briley	Bowgett	Cunningham	Ketteridge	Parsons 1	Leslie 1	Cork	Knowles	Galliers
25	Southend United	H	0-1	4,273	Goddard	Perkins	Jones	Galliers	Bowgett	Cunningham	Ketteridge	Parsons	Leslie	Cork	Knowles	Briley (10)
29	Orient (FLC2:1)	A	2-2	4,964	Goddard	Perkins	Jones	Galliers	Bowgett	Cunningham	Ketteridge	Parsons 1	Leslie 1	Downes	Knowles	Briley
Sept. 1	Blackpool	A	0-3	4,556	Goddard	Perkins	Jones	Galliers	Bowgett	Cunningham	Ketteridge	Parsons	Leslie	Downes	Knowles	Briley
4	Orient (FLC2:2)	H	2-2	3,702	Goddard	Perkins	Jones	Galliers	Bowgett	Cunningham	Ketteridge	Parsons 1	Leslie	Downes 1	Knowles	Briley
8	Blackburn Rovers	H	1-0	3,786	Goddard	Perkins	Jones	Galliers	Bowgett	Cunningham	Briley	Parsons	Leslie	Downes	Knowles 1	Denny (7)
15	Plymouth Argyle	A	0-3	5,744	Goddard	Perkins	Jones	Galliers	Bowgett	Haverson	Leslie	Parsons	Denny	Cork	Knowles	Downes
18	Gillingham	A	0-1	8,074	Goddard	Perkins	Jones	Galliers	Bowgett	Cunningham	Richards	Parsons	Downes	Cork	Knowles	Haverson
22	Brentford	H	0-0	5,524	Goddard	Perkins	Jones	Galliers	Bowgett	Cunningham	Richards	Parsons	Downes	Cork	Knowles	Leslie (11)
26	Plymouth Argyle (FLC3)	A	0-0	6,090	Goddard	Perkins	Downes	Galliers	Bowgett	Cunningham	Richards	Parsons	Leslie	Cork	Knowles	Dziadulewicz
29	Bury	A	2-1	2,790	Goddard	Perkins	Jones	Galliers	Bowgett	Cunningham	Ketteridge 1	Parsons	Leslie 1	Cork	Lewington	Dziadulewicz
Oct. 2	Plymouth (FLC3 Rply)	H	1-0	5,042	Goddard	Perkins	Jones	Galliers	Bowgett	Cunningham	Ketteridge	Parsons	Leslie 1	Cork	Lewington	Dziadulewicz (4)
6	Carlisle United	A	1-1	4,476	Goddard	Perkins	Jones	Galliers	Bowgett	Cunningham 1	Ketteridge	Parsons	Leslie	Cork	Lewington	Dziadulewicz (9)
9	Exeter City	H	2-2	2,990	Goddard	Perkins	Jones	Galliers	Bowgett	Cunningham	Ketteridge	Parsons	Leslie 1	Cork	Lewington	Dziadulewicz
13	Swindon Town	H	2-0	4,195	Goddard	Perkins	Jones	Ketteridge	Bowgett	Cunningham	Dziadulewicz	Parsons	Leslie	Cork 2	Lewington	Downes
20	Chesterfield	A	0-0	5,122	Goddard	Perkins	Jones	Downes	Bowgett	Cunningham	Ketteridge	Parsons	Dziadulewicz	Cork	Lewington	Richards
23	Colchester United	A	0-4	4,396	Goddard	Perkins	Jones	Eames	Bowgett	Cunningham	Dziadulewicz	Parsons	Leslie	Cork	Lewington	Ketteridge (8)
27	Sheffield Wed.	H	3-4	6,009	Goddard	Perkins	Jones	Galliers	Bowgett	Cunningham	Ketteridge	Parsons 1	Leslie 1	Cork 1	Lewington	Dziadulewicz (7)
30	Swindon Town (FLC4)	H	1-2	7,478	Goddard	Perkins 1	Jones	Galliers	Bowgett	Cunningham	Dziadulewicz	Parsons	Leslie	Cork	Lewington	Denny
Nov. 3	Chester	A	1-3	2,891	Goddard	Eames	Jones	Galliers	Bowgett	Cunningham	Dziadulewicz	Parsons	Leslie	Cork	Lewington	Denny (9)
6	Colchester United	H	3-3	2,425	Goddard	Eames	Jones	Galliers	Bowgett	Downes	Dziadulewicz	Parsons 2	Leslie 1	Cork	Lewington	Denny
10	Rotherham United	H	0-1	2,798	Goddard	Briley	Jones	Galliers	Bowgett	Downes	Dziadulewicz	Parsons	Leslie	Cork	Lewington	Eames
17	Grimsby Town	A	0-1	6,716	Goddard	Briley	Jones	Galliers	Bowgett	Downes	Dziadulewicz	Parsons	Leslie	Cork	Lewington	Ketteridge (2)
24	Gillingham (FAC1)	A	0-0	7,027	Goddard	Briley	Jones	Galliers	Bowgett	Cunningham	Dziadulewicz	Parsons	Leslie	Cork	Lewington	Downes (9)
27	Gillingham (FAC1 R.)	H	4-2	4,612	Goddard	Briley	Jones	Galliers	Bowgett	Downes	Dziadulewicz 1	Parsons 1	Leslie 2	Cork	Lewington	Denny (9)
Dec. 1	Hull City	A	1-1	3,750	Goddard	Briley	Jones	Galliers	Bowgett	Downes	Dziadulewicz	Parsons	Leslie	Cork 1	Lewington	Ketteridge
8	Sheffield United	H	1-1	4,785	Goddard	Briley	Jones	Galliers	Bowgett	Downes	Dziadulewicz	Parsons	Leslie	Cork 1	Lewington	Denny
18	Portsmouth (FAC 2)	H	0-0	10,850	Goddard	Briley	Jones	Galliers	Bowgett	Downes	Dziadulewicz	Parsons	Denny	Cork	Lewington	Cunningham
24	Portsmouth (FAC 2 R.)	A	3-3	17,000	Goddard	Briley	Jones	Galliers	Bowgett	Downes	Dziadulewicz	Parsons	Denny 2	Cork	Lewington	Cunningham
29	Southend United	A	3-1	3,952	Goddard	Briley	Jones	Galliers	Bowgett	Downes	Dziadulewicz	Parsons	Denny 2	Cork 1	Lewington	Leslie (7)
Jan. 5	Portsmouth (FAC 2 R)	H	0-1	7,484	Goddard	Briley	Jones	Galliers	Bowgett	Cunningham	Perkins	Parsons	Denny	Cork	Lewington	Leslie (11)
12	Blackpool	H	1-2	2,688	Goddard	Briley	Jones	Galliers	Bowgett	Cunningham	Dziadulewicz	Parsons	Leslie	Cork	Lewington	Denny

19 Plymouth Argyle	H	3-1	3,488	Goddard	Briley	Jones	Galliers	Smith	Cunningham	Ketteridge	Parsons 1	Leslie 1	Cork	Lewington	Denny
23 Swindon Town	A	1-2	10,743	Goddard	Briley	Bowgett	Denny 1	Smith	Cunningham	Ketteridge	Parsons	Leslie	Cork	Lewington	Downes
26 Bury	H	0-1	3,038	Goddard	Briley	Bowgett	Galliers	Smith	Cunningham	Ketteridge	Parsons	Leslie	Cork	Lewington	Denny (3)
Mar. 1 Chesterfield	H	1-1	3,609	Goddard	Briley	Bowgett	Galliers	Smith	Cunningham	Ketteridge	Parsons 1	Leslie	Cork	Lewington	Denny
5 Reading	A	0-3	5,246	Goddard	Briley	Bowgett	Galliers	Smith	Cunningham	Denny	Parsons	Leslie	Cork	Ketteridge	Downes
8 Sheffield Wed.	A	1-3	20,803	Goddard	Briley	Jones	Galliers	Smith	Cunningham 1	Denny	Parsons	Leslie	Cork	Ketteridge	Downes (7)
11 Barnsley	H	1-2	2,785	Goddard	Briley	Jones	Galliers	Smith	Cunningham	Ketteridge 1	Dziadulewicz	Leslie	Cork	Downes	Denny
14 Carlisle United	H	0-0	2,093	Goddard	Denny	Jones	Galliers	Smith	Cunningham	Ketteridge	Dziadulewicz	Leslie	Cork	Downes	Bowgett
19 Oxford United	A	1-4	2,603	Goddard	Jones	Armstrong	Klug	Smith	Cunningham	Ketteridge 1	Dziadulewicz	Leslie	Cork	Downes	Denny
22 Rotherham United	A	0-0	3,810	Goddard	Downes	Armstrong	Klug	Smith	Cunningham	Ketteridge	Dziadulewicz	Leslie	Cork	Denny	Belfield
29 Grimsby Town	H	3-6	2,485	Goddard	Downes	Armstrong	Klug	Smith	Cunningham 1	Ketteridge	Dziadulewicz	Leslie 1	Cork	Denny 1	Driver (11)
Apr. 5 Millwall	A	2-2	5,354	Goddard	Jones	Downes	Klug	Smith	Cunningham	Ketteridge 1	Dziadulewicz	Leslie	Cork 1	Denny	Belfield (8)
7 Reading	H	1-1	4,198	Goddard	Downes	Bowgett	Klug	Smith	Cunningham	Ketteridge 1	Dziadulewicz	Leslie	Cork	Denny	Belfield
11 Barnsley	A	0-4	10,032	Goddard	Downes	Armstrong	Klug	Jones	Cunningham	Ketteridge	Dziadulewicz	Leslie	Cork	Denny	Galliers (8)
15 Oxford	H	1-3	2,256	Goddard	Downes	Jones	Galliers	Bowgett	Cunningham	Ketteridge	Klug	Leslie	Cork 1	Denny	Dziadulewicz
19 Hull City	H	3-2	2,046	Goddard	Downes	Jones	Galliers	Smith	Cunningham	Ketteridge	Klug	Leslie 2	Cork	Denny	Dziadulewicz (8)
22 Millwall	H	2-2	4,085	Goddard	Downes	Jones	Galliers	Smith	Cunningham	Ketteridge	Klug	Leslie	Cork 1	Denny	Dziadulewicz
26 Sheffield United	A	1-2	8,675	Goddard	Downes	Jones	Galliers	Smith	Cunningham	Ketteridge	Klug	Leslie	Cork	Denny	Dziadulewicz (8)
May 3 Mansfield Town	H	3-2	2,149	Goddard	Armstrong	Jones	Galliers 1	Bowgett	Cunningham 1	Ketteridge	Downes	Dziadulewicz	Cork 1	Denny	Klug

FINAL TABLE

LEAGUE DIVISION THREE

	P	W	D	L	F	A	W	D	L	F	A	Pts
Grimsby Town	46	18	2	3	46	16	8	8	7	27	26	62
Blackburn Rovers	46	13	5	5	34	17	12	4	7	24	19	59
Sheffield Wednesday	46	12	6	5	44	20	9	10	4	37	27	58
Chesterfield	46	16	5	2	46	16	7	6	10	25	30	57
Colchester United	46	10	10	3	39	20	10	2	11	25	36	52
Carlisle United	46	10	10	3	39	20	10	2	11	25	36	52
Reading	46	14	6	3	43	19	2	10	11	23	46	48
Exeter City	46	14	5	4	38	22	5	5	13	22	46	48
Chester	46	14	6	3	29	18	3	7	13	20	39	47
Swindon Town	46	15	4	4	50	20	4	4	15	21	43	46
Barnsley	46	10	7	6	29	20	6	7	10	24	36	46
Sheffield United	46	13	5	5	35	21	5	5	13	25	45	46
Rotherham United	46	13	4	6	38	24	5	6	12	20	42	41
Millwall	46	14	6	3	49	23	2	7	14	16	36	45
Plymouth Argyle	46	13	7	3	39	17	3	5	15	25	38	44
Gillingham	46	8	9	6	26	18	6	5	12	23	33	42
Oxford United	46	10	4	9	34	24	4	9	10	23	38	41
Blackpool	46	10	7	6	39	34	5	4	14	23	40	41
Brentford	46	10	6	7	33	26	5	5	13	26	47	41
Hull City	46	11	7	5	29	21	1	9	13	22	48	40
Bury	46	10	4	9	30	23	6	3	14	15	36	39
Southend United	46	11	6	6	33	23	3	4	16	14	35	38
Mansfield Town	46	9	9	5	31	24	1	7	15	16	34	36
WIMBLEDON	46	6	8	9	34	38	4	6	13	18	43	34

GOALS AND GAMES

APPEARANCES AND GOALSCORERS

	Appearances			Goals	
	Lge	Cup	Sub	Lge	Cup
Gary Armstrong	5				
Dave Beasant	2				
Micky Belfield			1		
Les Briley	20	7			
Paul Bowgett	30	12			
Alan Cork	41	10	1	12	1
Tommy Cunningham	39	9		5	
Paul Denny	19	3	4	3	2
Wally Downes	24	6	2	3	1
Phil Driver			1		
Mark Dziadulewicz	21	5	5	1	1
Terry Eames	3				
Steve Galliers	34	10	2	2	
Ray Goddard	44	12			
Paul Haverson	1				
Steve Jones	39	11			
Steve Ketteridge	32	5	2	6	
Brian Klug	10		1		
Ray Knowles	8	5		1	2
John Leslie	41	9	2	11	6
Ray Lewington	23	7			
Steve Parsons	33	12		7	4
Steve Perkins	15	8			1
Craig Richards	2	1			
Mick Smith	20				

Wimbledon FC 1979-80. Back row: Lee Harewood, Steve Jones, Paul Denny, Tommy Cunningham, Ray Goddard, Dave Beasant, Paul Bowgett, Steve Parsons, Alan Cork, Ray Knowles, Wally Downes, Terry Eames, John Leslie. Front row: Dario Gradi, Steve Ketteridge, Craig Richards, Ray Lewington, Steve Galliers, Les Briley, Steve Perkins, Paul Haverson, Mark Dziadunlewicz, Dave Bassett.

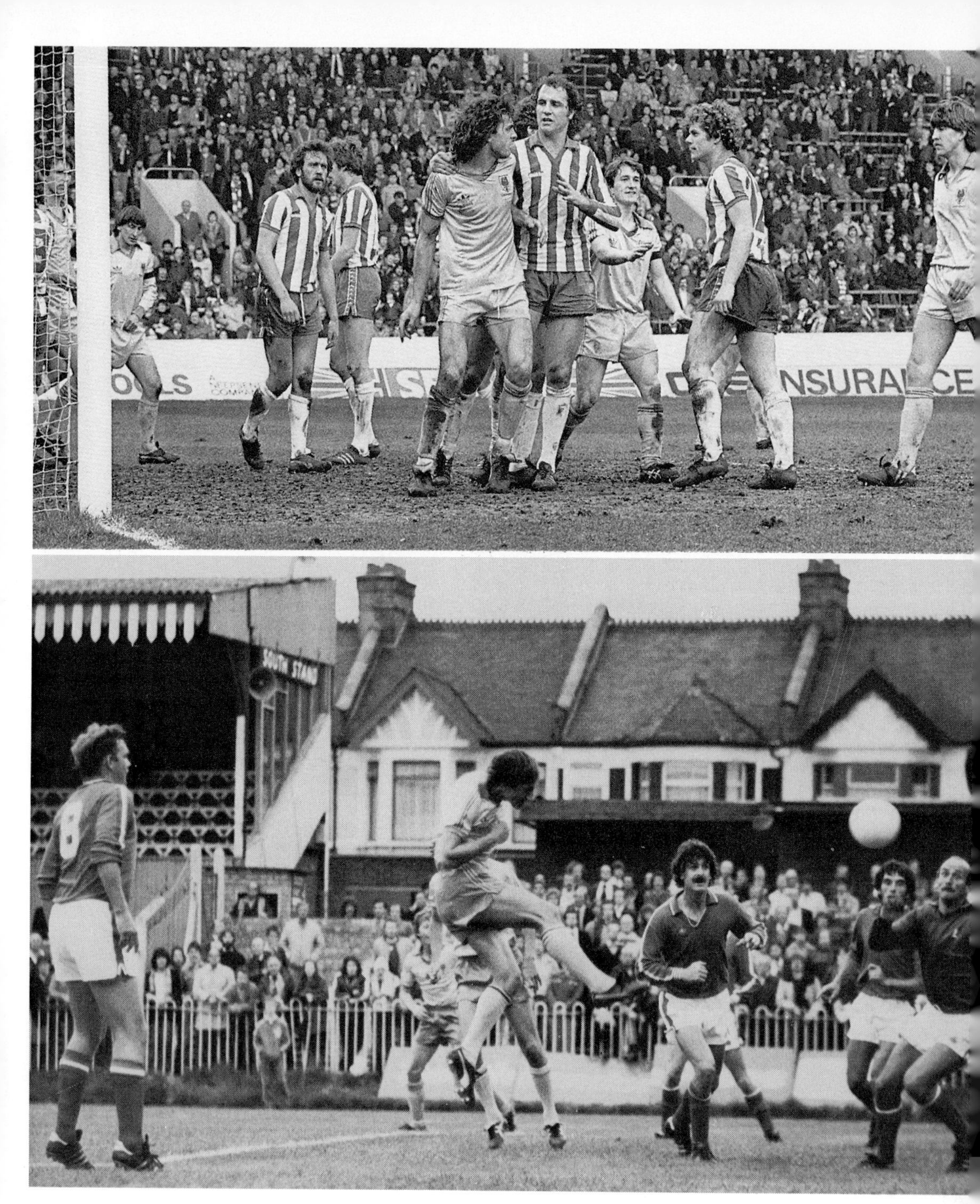

ABOVE: Andy McCulloch and Steve Galliers attempt to cool down Wimbledon's Steve Parsons and Wednesday's Ray Blackhall at Hillsborough in March 1980. BELOW: John Leslie heads Wimbledon's second goal during the 4-1 League Cup demolition of Aldershot.

Promotion Despite Turmoil 1980-81

A slow start

There was little close-season activity in the summer of 1980 as Wimbledon retained nearly all their squad from the previous campaign. Paul Bowgett and Craig Richards departed on free transfer as expected, and former Torquay man Roy Davies arrived – once again no fee was involved.

Davies made his debut in midfield in the 1st Round, 1st leg tie at Aldershot. On a boiling hot day, defensive errors allowed the Shots a 2-0 win. Back at Plough Lane for the second leg four days later, two John Leslie headers cancelled out the deficit within 32 minutes. Then an Alan Cork cross set up Paul Denny to put the Dons ahead in the tie for the first time. Aldershot pulled one back in the 66th minute but Wally Downes' low header with four minutes left saw Wimbledon through 4-3 on aggregate.

On the eve of the League campaign, Tommy Cunningham put in a transfer request. Gradi immediately announced that he would not be leaving unless the £45,000 fee the Club paid for him was recouped in full. This was the backdrop for the visit of Bradford City on the opening day of the season, who returned with a point from a 2-2 draw.

Depite being reduced to ten men late in the game, following injuries to both full backs Gary Armstrong and Steve Jones, Wimbledon came back to force a point. Bradford 'keeper Smith saved Wally Downes' injury time penalty but Downes was fastest to the rebound and lashed a shot over the grounded 'keeper.

'With reservations I thought we were brilliant,' commented Gradi afterwards. 'The reservations were that we didn't take our chances.' He was less positive after the midweek defeat at Aldershot. For the second time in ten days the Dons lost 2-0 at the Recreation Ground. Only Peter Brown, making his debut at right back, earned his praise.

Wimbledon seemed to have their minds on a League Cup meeting with Sheffield Wednesday, as they faced Port Vale in their next match. An Alan Cork header secured both points but it was an unconvincing display. Facing Wednesday on the following Tuesday the Dons were well worth the 2-1 win in the first leg of the 2nd Round tie. Goals from Cunningham and Leslie gave them a lead to take to Yorkshire.

Just four days later, two goals from winger Paul Driver gave Wimbledon their first away points of the season, in a 2-1 win at Scunthorpe. Then, despsite taking the lead, with an Alan Cork header, over 15,000 fans were able to cheer Sheffield Wednesday to a 3-1 second leg win, which sent the Dons out of the League Cup.

The low key start to the season continued at home to Stockport County, as a succession of missed chances left the Dons on the wrong end of a 2-1 scoreline. But a week later, Alan Cork's hat-trick set up a 3-0 win at Crewe Alexandra. The nucleus of a promotion-winning team was in place, but they lacked consistency.

At Gresty Road, Dave Beasant took Goddard's place in goal, holding the position until the final two months of the season. In front of him the Dons normally had Peter Brown and Gary Armstrong at full back, with Mick Smith and Tommy Cunningham in the centre. A midfield of Steve Galliers and Steve Ketteridge was supported by wingers Phil Driver and Wally Downes. Alan Cork and John Leslie were the potent, double strike force.

The young team — only John Leslie was over 25 — continued to lose as many games as it won. A narrow 1-0 defeat at Mansfield was followed by defeat on a similar scoreline at home to Lincoln City. Phil Driver's excellent form meant a £20,000 move to Chelsea, allowing Dave Hubbick, £5,000 from Ipswich Town, to come into the line-up for the first time at Halifax Town. It was his cross in the 73rd minute that John Leslie volleyed home to secure a welcome 1-0 win. It was announced after the match that John Leslie had signed a new three year contract, thus ending speculation about his future.

It was that man Leslie again who managed to break the deadlock 10 minutes from time, to ensure a 2-1 success in the return with Mansfield Town as the League action continued. Dave Hubbick celebrated his home debut, by giving the Dons the lead, with eight minutes to go before half-time. Terry Austin equalised within a minute only, for Leslie's snapshot from a narrow angle to secure the points.

Two more defeats — 3-0 at Tranmere and 1-0 at home to Southend — left Wimbledon in 14th place. Commenting on the Southend game, Gradi fumed: 'I'm not prepared to watch that sort of performance again. I will make my decisions on changes to the side in the cold light of day. But there will be changes . . .'

Off the field too, changes were threatened. Chairman Ron Noades claimed that the Borough did not want the Club, and that he was involved in talks to take Wimbledon to Milton Keynes!

The Milton Keynes Development Corporation had expressed an interest in the Plough Lane set-up and Noades, accompanied by fellow directors Jimmy Rose and Bernie Coleman, had been involved in preliminary talks. The problem, as always, was money, with the Borough's pre-emption value on the Plough Lane site of just £8,000 making it impossible to borrow.

Noades was also investigating other ventures, including Rugby League, or a move to Guildford. The moves came after the collapse of Golddigger Promotions 'Spot the Ball' competition, which left the Club with a bill for £20,000. The story was set to run and run.

LEFT: Peter Brown crosses the ball during the home defeat by Lincoln City. RIGHT: John Leslie fires over as future Don, Mick Harford, challenges. BELOW: Dave Hubbick (hidden by Mansfield's Derek Dawkins) scores his first goal for Wimbledon.

LEFT: Glyn Hodges, on his League debut, makes a perfect tackle on Hartlepool's Keith Houchen. BELOW: Alan Cork scores the second in the 3-0 win over York City. RIGHT: Alan Cork scores again! This time it is the winner against Northampton Town.

Finance or football?

As winter approached, Wimbledon were in mid-table and struggling to find any consistent form. So Gradi acted to make three changes for the visit of Hartlepool. Most notable was a debut for 17-year-old Glyn Hodges, a product of the youth team. Goals from Galliers, Cork, Ketteridge and two from John Leslie ensured a 5-0 win. Gradi's mood changed too. 'At times we were playing some terrific football, particularly in the build-ups to the goals', he beamed. 'We played well, within a pattern.'

The next week Wimbledon were one down in fifteen minutes at Hereford; however, the Dons came back for a 1-1 draw with only home 'keeper Brand denying them both points. But there was no joy at Rochdale three days later, as four bookings were added to a 2-0 defeat. Dario Gradi pledged to keep playing skilful football despite the dropped points. 'The problem is trying to find the right balance between playing nice football and being hard to beat,' he explained.

Fortunately, two successive wins followed to ensure that the pressure on Gradi was relieved. Despite having a temperature of 104°, John Leslie played and set up two goals in the 3-0 win at home to York. Leslie's header in the 38th minute was parried into the path of Glyn Hodges, who scored his first goal for the Club. Five minutes later Leslie's shot was too hot for goalkeeper Blackburn and Cork scored.

The Dons were in a comfortable 10th place after a remarkable 2-1 win over Peterborough. With two minutes to go it looked over, and some of the Plough Lane crowd left for home with the score at 1-0 to the visitors. Cork and Leslie struck late, to salvage those two points.

Once again events off the pitch dominated the thoughts of those who followed the Club. Chairman Ron Noades and three other directors — Jimmy Rose, Bernie Coleman and Sam Hammam — were voted onto the Board of Milton Keynes City FC. The Chairman stressed: 'This is a move by four directors of Wimbledon, and not Wimbledon itself. We're there in an advisory capacity and for long term investment'. But he warned: 'Unless the pre-emption is sorted out there is no future for us at Plough Lane. Milton Keynes as a town has long-term potential. It can support a multi-purpose sports stadium, the potential is there'.

Meanwhile Merton Council leader Harry Cowd acted quickly to head off any move to take the Club away from Wimbledon. He indicated that a site in the Wandle Valley could be used for a luxury sports complex, with part of it given over as Wimbledon FC's new home. He commented: 'Wimbledon F.C. could move here. It would be ideal for them and would solve any problems they might have with us over this pre-emption clause'.

Noades greeted the news with excitement. 'I'm absolutely delighted,' he enthused. 'We would have no objections to such a move at all. Obviously there would have to be a string of guarantees and a binding contract. But these are technical problems and can easily be overcome. Wimbledon F.C. is finally moving forwards.'

However, progress on the field ground to a halt. Wimbledon's visit to Doncaster's Belle Vue ground was marred by violent scenes midway through the second half. After Ketteridge was brought down from behind for a controversial penalty, Wimbledon's directors were showered with missiles, including beer cans. Cork equalised from the spot, only for Stuart Mell to score a late Doncaster winner.

The awayday disappointments continued. At Roots Hall in front of nearly 5,000 fans the Dons slumped to a second 1-0 defeat of the season against Southend. The

Essex side, top of the table, scored through Derek Spence in the 66th minute and Wimbledon could not find a way back into the match. The Plough Lane team were now 12th with 18 points from 19 games.

Once again, returning home saw an upturn in fortunes. Alan Cork's 10th goal of the season, stabbed home from a yard out, was enough to beat Northampton Town. Then Glyn Hodges starred in the 4-0 demolition of Aldershot. Gradi noted that Hodges' contribution made Wimbledon the 'most dangerous we've looked at free kicks and corners since Steve Parsons left'. Two from Tommy Cunningham and one each from Cork and Leslie ensured a convincing win.

The poor away form continued though; at Bradford a 2-0 defeat was stopped from being even worse when Dave Beasant saved Terry Dolan's second half penalty. However, the FA Cup provided a welcome distraction from the pressure of League football as non-League Windsor & Eton were beaten 7-2 at Plough Lane. A hat-trick from Dave Hubbick set the Dons on their way. Alan Cork scored his thirteenth goal of the season and announced that he was happy at the Club but he was not happy with the terms of his new contract. 'I'm one of the Club's longest serving players and I think I deserve a bit more than I am being offered.'

Meanwhile, Ron Noades and Merton Councillors met to discuss the £8,000 clause at Plough Lane. A joint statement issued after the meeting said that it was agreed that 'both the council and the football club would urgently consider all the issues raised and meet again early in the New Year'.

With only one point from their previous six away games, Wimbledon travelled to Bury. Paul Hilton's header ensured that it was another wasted journey. It was a turning point. In the eleven remaining away games, the Dons were beaten only twice. At home they were destined to lose only once — on the last day of the season. Clearly the imminent upheaval in the boardroom and a change of manager were the key reasons for this transformation, but the arrival of Francis Joseph, a £3,000 signing from Hillingdon Borough, was significant. He made his debut at home to Darlington in the next match. Coming on as substitute, he ensured a point with a 79th minute equaliser. But it was a poor performance by the side and one which cried out for the vision of the suspended Glyn Hodges.

Then a much improved performance took Wimbledon through to the 3rd Round of the FA Cup. Third Division Swindon Town were on the wrong end of a 2-0 scoreline. Dave Beasant was the hero, having been slammed by the manager during the week for letting in too many easy goals. 'Brilliant,' admitted Gradi. 'That was the bonus of a fine win, seeing just how good Dave was in that type of situation.'

The Dons were 2-0 up in twenty minutes, through Paul Denny and John Leslie, and then had to withstand a fierce onslaught from the Wiltshire side. Said Gradi: 'We fought well even though we panicked for most of the second half'.

The weather wiped out any other games before Christmas but the Dons ended the year on a winning note, by beating Torquay 3-2 on Boxing Day and Bournemouth 2-0 a day later. A refereeing performance from Clive Thomas at Plainmoor, in which he sent off John Leslie and booked three other Dons, could not take the spotlight away from an excellent display. Cork, Leslie and Hubbick were the scorers and against Bournemouth, Cork and Hubbick were on target again. As the new year approached the Dons could afford to be quietly optimistic.

ABOVE: A dream debut as substitute Francis Joseph fires home the equaliser against Darlington. BELOW: John Leslie prepares to score the second goal in the FA Cup victory over Swindon.

ABOVE: John Leslie holds off a challenge by Oldham's John Hurst during the 0-0 draw at Plough Lane. BELOW: Oldham 'keeper John Platt saves again as the Dons press forward.

Top team join Palace

There was little sign of the turmoil ahead, as January opened with the visit of Second Division Oldham to Plough Lane. Over four and a half thousand fans saw the FA Cup Third Round clash but Wimbledon could not finish off Athletic after Paul Futcher was sent off in the 29th minute. The replay in Lancashire three days later proved to be a wonderful triumph for the whole team. An inspired display of goalkeeping by Dave Beasant kept the home side at bay until the 86th minute. Then from Paul Denny's cross, Alan Cork fired home the only goal of the game.

Manager Dario Gradi, named Manager of the Month, savoured the triumph: 'A magnificent effort. My players did all they were asked to, and more. Oldham didn't get behind us once and apart from two Dave Beasant saves they didn't really threaten'. Skipper Steve Galliers paid tribute to the back four. 'They were terrific,' said Galliers; 'They stood there and took all that Oldham had to offer.'

The news that the next home game with Rochdale was postponed due to bad weather was overshadowed by rumours that Ron Noades was about to take control at Selhurst Park. Palace Chairman Ray Bloye was believed to be ready to sell Noades 12,933 shares — a controlling interest. Noades and Bloye both refused to comment.

Back on the field Wimbledon preserved their unbeaten home record, stretching over three months, with a last gasp equaliser against Scunthorpe. On 19 January Steve Galliers powered a loose ball through a flurry of legs with literally the last kick of the game, to ensure a 2-2 draw. The deal with Palace was now out in the open and the plans involved the two clubs sharing a ground at Selhurst Park.

The fans were outraged and expressed their views forcibly in the *Wimbledon News*. Charlie Addiman, a supporter for many years, expressed the views of many: 'If I wanted to go to Selhurst Park I would have done so when Palace were in the First Division rather than watch Wimbledon in the Isthmian League. I would support any team that played at Plough Lane, regardless of status, rather than go to the Palace'.

Ron Noades offered his personal guarantee that Wimbledon could stay at Plough Lane — until the end of the season! 'An average crowd of 2,200 will not keep Wimbledon from going under,' he said. 'but if 3,500 turned up it would be a different story.'

The proposed deal was as follows: a holding company would be set up that owned both grounds. The two clubs would stay as separate concerns, each with their own boards and management. Selhurst Park, would be used as the football stadium and Plough Lane redeveloped as a sports complex.

'We feel sorry that 2,000 supporters should suffer just because the rest of the Borough doen't want us,' said Noades. 'We can decide at the end of the season on any changes and be ready for next season.' He promised that coaches would take supporters to Selhurst Park on match days.

The large contingent of Wimbledon fans in Wrexham for the FA Cup Fourth Round tie made their feeelings on the proposals plain. Any move to take Wimbledon away from Plough Lane would be strongly opposed. On the pitch Wimbledon quickly went 2-0 down but fought back with a Paul Denny header in the 69th minute. Despite late chances the Dons bowed out, their heads held high after a 2-1 defeat.

The weeks following the FA Cup-tie were momentous. Ron Noades became Chairman of Crystal Palace and took Dario Gradi with him to Selhurst Park to become team manager. Dave Bassett took over as boss at Plough Lane and was immediately upbeat about the team's chances. 'We've got an outside chance of going up,' he said, 'but there is no room for a slip-up. We can't get away with winning one and drawing the other two of our games in hand because that just won't do. One upset and we're out of it.'

Wimbledon supporters launched a fund-raising scheme to keep the Club in SW19. Consortium boss Ron Noades said that £150,000 would buy his shares in Wimbledon FC. Over 300 supporters attended an angry meeting and fans vowed to contact local firms and businesses to raise the cash.

The key to the long-term future lay with Sam Hammam. He had not returned from a business trip to Saudi Arabia, but his one-third holding in Wimbledon FC was not tied in any way to the Palace takeover. If he wanted Wimbledon to say put and Noades shares could be bought, the Club could have a future in Wimbledon.

New Chairman Joe McElligott outlined the best way forward. He explained that, if the average crowd were to rise to 3,500, then 'the new board can get at least another season at Plough Lane'.

Supporters Club Committee member — and Wimbledon director — Peter Cork coined the phrase 'Each one reach one' in his bid to get regular supporters to bring one friend each to Plough Lane. It offered some hope during those dark days.

Alan Cork slams home the first goal, from the spot, against Scunthorpe.

ABOVE: In the last minute, Steve Galliers beats Scunthorpe's Joe Neenan to make the score 2-2. BELOW: John Leslie (No 9) heads the first goal in the 2-1 victory over Tranmere Rovers.

LEFT: Mick Smith volleys over with the Tranmere 'keeper, Dick Johnson, well beaten. RIGHT: Steve Ketteridge battles for midfield supremacy in the home game with Torquay. BELOW: Steve Galliers is mobbed by delighted fans after the 4-1 win over Rochdale has ensured promotion.

An amazing late run

The Bassett era got off to a perfect start on 31 January with a 3-2 win at Port Vale. Mick Smith scored the winner, with a searing left foot volley after 75 minutes. Manager Dave Bassett was buoyant. 'It could not have been better. We attacked, we entertained and we scored goals. We also won, and it's really satisfying when all those things go together.'

It was the start of a run of eighteen games which included only two defeats, and carried the Dons into the Third Division. But at that stage events off field dominated. Supporters travelled by coach to Lytham St Anne's on the following Monday to protest to the Football League management committee about Noades' plans.

Following this, over 200 fans staged a peaceful sit-down protest on the terraces after the 2-0 win over Crewe. The crowd was up – but only by 500 – to around 2,700. Wimbledon director Doug Miller commented: 'We are all encouraged by that rise, but it must be consistent'.

Bassett was pleased to win the game but disappointed by the performance. Two goals from Alan Cork were enough 'but although the overall performance wasn't good, it was good enough to stop Crewe,' Bassett commented.

The next Friday night a 0-0 draw at Stockport left the Dons in 9th place with 35 points from 30 games. The fourth placed team – Doncaster Rovers – were only four points ahead and Wimbledon had three games in hand. Ron Noades handed over control of the Club to the new Board while retaining his 4,000 shares. 'I'm having no part in Wimbledon,' he said. 'They will make their own decisions.'

The new Board issued a statement on 18 February: 'After careful consideration, the new Wimbledon Board has decided not to play first team matches at the ground of Crystal Palace F.C. The Board are resolved in maintaining the Club's independence in all respects'. The statement went on to say that the future financial stability of the Club depended on Merton Council raising the pre-emption value of the ground.

Wimbledon's improved form under Bassett turned attention away from the off the field wranglings. Alan Cork's 20th goal of the season put the seal on a 3-0 win over Halifax Town. Cork and Dave Beasant were now being watched by scouts from a number of clubs. Representatives of Norwich, Chelsea, West Ham, Brentford, Brighton, Swindon and Leeds were at Plough Lane for the match.

Crucial matches followed. Precious points at fellow promotion chasers Lincoln and Peterborough were earned in the space of four days. Lincoln, lying second, had hoped to complete a double over the Dons, but a brave defensive display ensured the match was goalless. At London Road an Alan Cork equaliser with four minutes left pushed Wimbledon up into eighth place.

John Leslie's 13th goal of the season – but his first in 1981 – equalised an early Tranmere effort when Wimbledon returned to Plough Lane. Glyn Hodges scored the winner with only eight minutes left. A few days later, the transfer deadline passed with no movement either in or out.

Two consecutive visits to the North East followed and produced contrasting results. At Hartlepool the Dons were 3-0 up in 70 minutes, with two from Cork and a third from Wally Downes. But then the team relaxed, allowing the home side to storm back, and only Mick Smith kicking the ball off the line late on prevented an equaliser.

The four month unbeaten run ended at Feethams Crescent, Darlington. Tommy Cunningham and Steve Galliers were both sent off in a 4-1 defeat. The sensational double dismissal came 10 minutes from the end, as the pair argued with the referee over a controversial third goal. Both were adamant that the ball was out of play before being crossed for the goal but, having earlier been booked, they were both on thin ice.

'Players have got to learn to keep their mouths shut,' moaned Dons boss Bassett. 'I would rather not comment on the referee, but they were only protesting. The referee overreacted. He didn't understand the emotions or feelings. He spoilt a good game.' Wimbledon were now in sixth place.

On 22 March an experiment with Sunday soccer was partially successful. A bumper 3,898 crowd turned up at Plough Lane but the 0-0 draw with Hereford was a disappointment. 'Shocking,' was Dave Bassett's comment. 'Apart from John Leslie we had nothing up front, while the midfield didn't show either. It wasn't poor, it was abysmal.'

Without Dave Beasant — broken finger — and Steve Galliers — suspended for reaching 49 disciplinary points — the Dons won the next three games 1-0. Hodges' header was enough to beat Wigan at home, while Cork's 25th of the season saw off York at Bootham Crescent. That win moved the Dons into the promotion frame for the first time.

An inspired performance by Ray Goddard helped Wimbledon to a 1-0 home win over Doncaster. The victory saw them leapfrog the Yorkshire side into third place. Goddard had yet to concede a goal since his recall three games earlier. Doncaster player-manager Billy Bremner produced a brilliant display as sweeper in his last visit to London, but even he could not stop Alan Cork scoring his 26th of the season.

Dave Bassett remained calm. 'If we win our last six games we are up, regardless of what anyone else does,' he said. 'We shall continue to take each game as it comes, and nothing is going to be easy.' His Manager of the Month award was well deserved as Wimbledon's impressive run continued.

Micky Belfield made his full debut in place of Glyn Hodges at the County Ground, Northampton in the next match. The Dons did just enough to earn a 1-1 draw. Then two more 1-0 wins pushed the side to the brink of a coveted promotion place.

A large travelling contingent celebrated Wally Downes' winner on Easter Saturday in Bournemouth; and a Tommy Cunningham header was enough for a home win over Torquay on the Monday. 'This has been a remarkable run,' said Bassett. 'While other sides have felt the pressure and cracked, we've managed to keep getting the results.' Dave Beasant, back from injury, ensured the second win with two memorable saves.

Two points from three games were needed. However, a tired performance at Wigan meant that the Dons had to wait three more days to celebrate promotion. A 1-0 defeat could have been worse but Beasant was once again at his best. The promotion party was able to begin once two goals from John Leslie had ensured the 4-1 win over Rochdale.

A remarkable season was rounded off with a 4-2 defeat by mid-table Bury. Kevin Gage made his debut for the Dons but Ray Goddard, in his last League game, was the star. His 63rd minute penalty kick beat Neville Southall to record the first goal in a 479 game career.

The front cover of the programme issued for the Peterborough match.

ABOVE: Alan Cork bursts through despite the attentions of a Wrexham defender. BELOW: Mick Smith wins this aerial duel with Peterborough's Kellock.

Memorable Matches 1980-81

28 October 1980: FOOTBALL LEAGUE DIVISION FOUR

Wimbledon 2 *Leslie, Cork*

Peterborough 1 *Quow*

This match produced one of the most dramatic finishes ever seen at Plough Lane. In an amazing last two minutes, the Dons moved from one down to securing both points. The finale left the crowd breathless and boss Gradi enthusing: 'The fight back was brilliant'.

After a first half enlivened only by Peter Brown's penalty miss — his 30th minute kick hit a post — the second half proved far more exciting. The Dons' Dave Hubbick and Boro's Dave Syrett both missed open goal opportunities before Posh took the lead after 73 minutes. Live wire midfield man Trevor Quow fired home from 18 yards after a sweeping move.

That appeared to be that. With the crowd beginning to drift away and Peterborough playing out time, it appeared the Dons were heading for another home defeat. But Steve Galliers would have none of it. He drove Wimbledon forward and finally the pressure paid off, when John Leslie fired home from an acute angle with only two minutes left.

From the restart Glyn Hodges won the ball and threated it down the wing for the dynamic Galliers to run onto. He took it to the line at the Wandle end and pulled back a low cross. Steve Ketteridge went in for the ball at the near post and, although Keith Waugh blocked his shot, Alan Cork followed up to fire a last minute winner under the 'keeper's body.

The match was part of a period of transition for the Club, both on and off the pitch. Reports were appearing in the press over the problems between the Club and the Council regarding the pre-emption clause. On the playing side Dario Gradi's team was inconsistent, trying to play skilful football in a Division more suited to less subtle approaches.

The win left Wimbledon in 10th place with seven wins and seven defeats from sixteen matches. It was only after the turmoil of the new year — with Chairman and manager departing for Crystal Palace — that a consistent run was put together. It was then that new boss Dave Bassett's more pragmatic approach began to pay off and the Dons moved up into the promotion frame.

In hindsight, the Club owe both Ron Noades and Dario Gradi a great debt. Undoubtedly they were both significant factors in the Dons acclimatising to their new Football League surroundings so quickly. Equally, their departure in early 1981 paved the way for the dynamic duo of Hammam and Bassett to elevate the Club still further.

After this match Gradi proved to be in prophetic mood. 'Steve Galliers was a superman out there,' he commented. 'He would be able to play in the First Division without a doubt. He covered the entire pitch and tackled everyone'. Just six years later, as Wimbledon made their debut in Division One, Steve Galliers was there — wearing a Dons shirt.

WIMBLEDON: Beasant, Brown, Armstrong, Galliers, Smith, Cunningham, Ketteridge, Hodges, Leslie, Cork, Hubbick. Sub: Jones.

PETERBOROUGH: Waugh, Winters, Robson, Hodgson, Slough, Foster, Quow, Kellock, Cooke, Syrett, Gallagher (Guy).

CROWD: 1,901 REFEREE: Mr D. Letts (Basingstoke)

24 January 1981: FA Cup 4th ROUND
Wrexham 2 *Fox, McNeil*
Wimbledon 1 *Denny*

Having disposed of Windsor, Swindon and Oldham to reach this tie, all attention should have been focused on events on the field of play. In fact Wimbledon's large band of travelling supporters was more concerned about whether the Club would survive at all.

News of Ron Noades' plan to take over Crystal Palace and force the two clubs to share Selhurst Park had leaked out. Most fans saw it as a first step towards an eventual merger, with the smaller club, Wimbledon, effectively disappearing.

The travelling army made their feelings known with banners and chants directed at the directors' box. On the field the Dons were showing scant respect for their Second Division opponents. With Tommy Cunningham and Steve Galliers in dominant mood, Wimbledon had taken an early strangehold on proceedings.

Steve Jones was causing problems with a string of foraging runs, while Cork was only a fraction offside as he turned home Glyn Hodges' through ball in the 32nd minute. But four minutes later Wrexham took the lead against the run of play after Ian Edwards laid the ball off, for Mel Sutton to cross from the right. Steve Fox reacted quickest to beat Beasant with a low shot from 10 yards.

Wrexham went 2-0 up in the 58th minute, following a free kick conceded when Galliers brought down Fox on the edge of the box. Goal ace Dixie McNeil was allowed an unchallenged header from Les Cartwright's free kick with Beasant rooted to his line.

The Dons hit back in the 69th minute. Wally Downes crossed from the right and Paul Denny — back to goal and some 15 yards out — looped a header over Welsh International goalkeeper Dai Davies into the top corner.

Three minutes later, left back Dave Armstrong freed Alan Cork down the wing. His deep cross was met at the far post by Steve Jones but his volley went harmlessly wide. Glyn Hodges was withdrawn, after being barracked by a section of the crowd, and Dave Hubbick came on to replace him.

He was immediately in the action. Steve Ketteridge and Alan Cork exchanged passes to put Hubbick through into the 18 yard box. With the whole goal to aim at, he succeeded only in hitting the goalkeeper's body. Then, with two minutes left and Dons continually pushing forward, a long punt from Beasant put him clear once again. The ball would not come down fast enough and Joey Jones got back to force a corner.

There was no disguising Hubbick's upset afterward. 'It will take me longer than this weekend to get over that first miss,' he said. 'It's the other players I feel sorry for; they had battled hard and there was I with the chance to give them their reward.'

Wrexham's player coach Mel Sutton was clearly relieved when the final whistle blew. 'We really needed that two goal cushion,' he said. 'I was surprised at how well Wimbledon came back at us.' So the Dons were out of the Cup for that year; the supporters waited and wondered if the Club would exist next year.

WREXHAM: Davies, Hill, Kenworthy, Jones J., Cegielski, Arkwright, Fox, Sutton, Edwartds, McNeil, Cartwright.

WIMBLEDON: Beasant, Jones, Armstrong, Galliers, Smith, Cunningham, Ketteridge, Hodges (Hubbick), Denny, Cork, Downes.

CROWD: 12,267 REFEREE: Mr J. Hunting (Leics)

4 April 1981: FOOTBALL LEAGUE DIVISION FOUR
Wimbledon 1 *Cork*
Doncaster Rovers 0

After weeks spent edging up the table, this was the match that moved the Dons from promotion possible to probables. The Yorkshire side, among the front runners all season, were swept aside by a hard-working Wimbledon performance. The two points gained saw Bassett's men leapfrog Rovers into third place.

However, it was 37-year-old Doncaster boss Billy Bremner who stole the headlines. Playing at sweeper, in his only full game of the season, he orchestrated his side's second half revival. It only floundered on the rock of Ray Goddard, 32-years-young, in the Wimbledon goal, who stopped dangerous efforts from Warboys, Harle and Glyn Snodin. It turned out to be the final full match of Bremner's illustrious career.

Bremner needed all his calm authority in an opening spell which Wimbledon dominated. Centre back Mick Smith twice went close with headers and midfield man Steve Ketteridge fired a volley just over.

But it was Smith who almost let in the much travelled Doncaster striker Alan Warboys after 26 minutes. In attempting to head a clearance back to Ray Goddard, he allowed Warboys to steal in behind him. Only a timely intervention from Tommy Cunningham averted the danger.

Four minutes later Wimbledon took a deserved lead. Young Glyn Hodges delivered a perfect cross from the left and Smith rose highest to nod the ball down. With Bremner for once out of position, Alan Cork was able to fire the ball home from five yards for his 26th goal of the season.

The Dons continued to create chances during a tense second half but it was Doncaster who were generally in control. Ray Goddard demonstrated just why he was keeping young Dave Beasant out of the team, with a string of fine saves. Indeed it was Goddard's fourth clean sheet in a row, since coming into the side after the Darlington debacle.

Peter Brown, replacing the injured Steve Jones at right back, had a fine game, and tested goalkeeper Boyd with a 30 yard drive early in the second half.

Wimbledon manager Dave Bassett praised his opposite number afterwards, indicating that speed of foot was no substitute for speed of thought in football. He acknowledged that it had been a close thing. 'We needed a second goal to relax,' he commented afterwards, 'but it just wouldn't come. It was a tense game played between two good sides'.

Sixteen-year-old Kevin Gage was the home substitute but did not make his debut. He had to wait a few months to become the youngest player to appear for the Dons in the Football League.

WIMBLEDON: Goddard, Brown, Armstrong, Denny, Smith, Cunningham, Ketteridge, Hodges, Leslie, Cork, Downes; Sub: Gage (not used).
DONCASTER ROVERS: Boyd, Russell, Bremner, Snodin, I., Swan, Lister, Pugh, Aldridge, Warboys, Snodin, G., Harle.
CROWD: 3,595 REFEREE: Mr L. Burden (Dorset)

28 April 1981: FOOTBALL LEAGUE DIVISION FOUR
Wimbledon 4 *Leslie 2, Hodges, Galliers*
Rochdale 1 *Wann*

Mid-table and out of the Cups when Dave Bassett took over in late January, this match assured Wimbledon of promotion following an amazing late surge. It was Bassett's eighteenth in charge and in that time his team had recorded eleven wins and five draws. The success was even more remarkable set against a season of speculation, boardroom drama and managerial walk-outs.

It was John Leslie who was the hero of the hour. With just one goal in 1981 before the game, he scored twice in the first eleven minutes to set the Dons on their way. He volleyed home on the turn after five minutes — an excellent goal. Then he latched on to Dave Beasant's huge clearance downfield, to shoot on the run past Graeme Crawford in the Rochdale goal.

Despite this contribution goalkeeper Beasant was at fault as the Lancastrians replied four minutes from half time. Dennis Wann's low free kick squirmed through his fingers to make the score 2-1 at the break. Beasant made amends when he turned another Wann piledriver around the post after 54 minutes, but soon the action switched to the other end.

Steve Galliers ran from inside his own half to set up the third goal. His final shot was pushed away by Crawford, towards the right edge on the penalty area. The first player to react was Steve Ketteridge, whose 75th minute chip was met by a powerful Glyn Hodges header, which put the result beyond doubt.

It was fitting that Galliers should have the final word three minutes later. His contribution to the match and to the Dons' season was immense. With Wimbledon knocking the ball around with huge confidence, he finished off a fine passing movement with a low drive into the corner of the net.

The Dons were now completely on top and, with the crowd coming over the fences ready to invade the pitch, Wally Downes hit the bar with a chip from the right wing. Finally the whistle went, and the players made a dash for the safety of the dressing room, as the supporters ran onto the turf. They returned to salute their fans as the celebrations began in earnest. A jubilant Bassett was euphoric after the epic win. He commented: 'We had a little anxious spell when we gave them a silly goal, but didn't we finish in style?'

'Dario Gradi and Ron Noades leaving didn't affect us. We spoke about it and decided we had a job to do and then got on and did it. We're better equipped this time than when we went up before, in terms of experience and playing strength. I've got a lot of faith in these players.'

After all the traumas of the previous six months, promotion was a remarkable achievement. Money was so tight that Bassett had to rely entirely on the personnel he inherited from Gradi. The beginnings of the 'long ball' style, for which Wimbledon were to become famous, were also evident as he changed the more measured short passing approach favoured by his predecessor.

Bassett later commented that promotion had come so easily he considered football management had few problems. He came to realise, in 12 months, just how hard it was.

WIMBLEDON: Beasant, Brown, Armstrong (Hodges), Galliers, Smith, Cunningham, Ketteridge, Denny, Leslie, Joseph, Downes.

ROCHDALE: Crawford, Jones, Snookes, Weir, Burke, Taylor, Wann, O'Loughlin, Hilditch, Wellings, Martinez.

CROWD: 3,884 REFEREE: Mr C. Shapter (Torquay)

ABOVE: Paul Denny's looping header pulls one goal back to set up a grand finale at Wrexham. BELOW: Billy Bremner appeals successfully and Mick Smith's headed 'goal' is disallowed.

ABOVE: Alan Cork and Glyn Snodin in a dance. BELOW: Paul Denny and Rochdale's Barry Wellings tussle for this ball.

ABOVE: John Leslie fires home his second goal in the 4-1 demolition of Rochdale. BELOW: Steve Ketteridge fires a shot just wide during the Cup-tie with Swindon in December 1980.

1980 - 81 AT A GLANCE

DATE	OPPONENTS	H/A	Res.	Att.	1	2	3	4	5	6	7	8	9	10	11	12
Aug. 9	Aldershot (FLC1:1)	A	0-2	3,023	Goddard	Jones	Armstrong	Galliers	Smith	Cunningham	Ketteridge	Downes	Leslie	Cork	Davies	Denny (7)
12	**Aldershot (FLC1:2)**	H	4-1	2,444	Goddard	Jones	Armstrong	Galliers	Smith	Cunningham	Ketteridge	Downes 1	Leslie 2	Cork	Denny 1	Davies
16	**Bradford City**	H	2-2	2,161	Goddard	Jones	Armstrong	Galliers	Smith	Cunningham	Ketteridge	Downes 1	Leslie	Cork 1	Denny	Davies (3)
19	Aldershot	A	0-2	2,922	Goddard	Brown	Perkins	Galliers	Smith	Cunningham	Ketteridge	Downes	Leslie	Cork	Denny	Davies
23	**Port Vale**	H	1-0	1,775	Goddard	Brown	Perkins	Galliers	Smith	Cunningham	Ketteridge	Downes	Leslie	Cork 1	Driver	Davies (7)
26	**Sheffield Wednesday (FLC 2)**	A	2-1	3,549	Goddard	Brown	Perkins	Galliers	Smith	Cunningham	Davies	Downes	Leslie 1	Cork	Driver	Armstrong
30	Scunthorpe United	A	2-1	1,624	Goddard	Brown	Perkins	Galliers	Smith	Cunningham	Davies	Downes	Leslie	Cork	Driver 2	Armstrong
Sept. 2	Sheffield Wednesday (FLC 2)	A	1-3	15,151	Goddard	Brown	Perkins	Galliers	Smith	Cunningham	Davies	Downes	Leslie	Cork 1	Driver	Armstrong
6	**Stockport County**	H	1-2	2,010	Goddard	Brown	Perkins	Galliers	Smith	Cunningham	Davies	Downes	Leslie 1	Cork	Driver	Denny (7)
13	Crewe Alexandra	A	3-0	1,881	Beasant	Brown	Perkins	Galliers	Smith	Cunningham	Denny	Downes	Leslie	Cork 3	Armstrong	Driver (5)
15	Mansfield Town	A	0-1	2,950	Beasant	Brown	Armstrong	Galliers	Perkins	Cunningham	Denny	Downes	Leslie	Cork	Driver	Smith (8)
20	**Lincoln City**	H	0-1	2,380	Beasant	Perkins	Armstrong	Galliers	Smith	Cunningham	Denny	Downes	Leslie	Cork	Brown	Davies
27	Halifax Town	A	1-0	1,407	Beasant	Brown	Perkins	Galliers	Smith	Cunningham	Davies	Downes	Leslie 1	Cork	Hubbick	Hodges (11)
30	**Mansfield Town**	H	2-1	2,052	Beasant	Brown	Perkins	Galliers	Smith	Downes	Ketteridge	Davies	Leslie 1	Cork	Hubbick 1	Armstrong
Oct. 3	Tranmere Rovers	A	0-3	2,507	Beasant	Brown	Perkins	Galliers	Smith	Cunningham	Davies	Downes	Leslie	Cork	Hubbick	Ketteridge 8
7	**Southend United**	H	0-1	2,117	Beasant	Brown	Perkins	Galliers	Smith	Cunningham	Davies	Downes	Leslie	Cork	Hubbick	Hodges (7)
11	**Hartlepool United**	H	5-0	1,971	Beasant	Brown	Armstrong	Galliers 1	Smith	Cunningham	Ketteridge 1	Hodges	Leslie 2	Cork 1	Hubbick	Perkins
18	Hereford United	A	1-1	2,369	Beasant	Brown	Armstrong	Galliers	Smith	Cunningham	Ketteridge	Hodges	Leslie	Cork	Hubbick 1	Jones
21	Rochdale	A	0-2	2,391	Beasant	Brown	Armstrong	Galliers	Smith	Cunningham	Ketteridge	Hodges	Leslie	Cork	Hubbick	Jones
25	**York City**	H	3-0	2,082	Beasant	Brown	Armstrong	Galliers	Smith	Cunningham	Ketteridge	Hodges 1	Leslie	Cork 1	Hubbick	Jones (9)
28	**Peterborough United**	H	2-1	1,901	Beasant	Brown	Armstrong	Galliers	Smith	Cunningham	Ketteridge	Hodges	Leslie 1	Cork 1	Hubbick	Jones
Nov. 1	Doncaster Rovers	A	1-2	3,245	Beasant	Brown	Armstrong	Galliers	Smith	Cunningham	Ketteridge	Hodges	Leslie	Cork 1	Hubbick	Jones
3	Southend United	A	0-1	4,935	Beasant	Brown	Armstrong	Galliers	Smith	Cunningham	Ketteridge	Hodges	Leslie	Cork	Hubbick	Jones (11)
8	**Northampton Town**	H	1-0	2,029	Beasant	Jones	Armstrong	Downes	Smith	Cunningham	Ketteridge	Hodges	Leslie	Cork 1	Hubbick	Brown (11)
11	**Aldershot**	H	4-0	2,538	Beasant	Jones	Armstrong	Denny	Smith	Cunningham 2	Ketteridge	Hodges	Leslie 1	Cork 1	Hubbick	Downes
15	Bradford City	A	0-2	3,327	Beasant	Jones	Armstrong	Denny	Smith	Cunningham	Ketteridge	Hodges	Leslie	Cork	Hubbick	Brown (11)
22	**Windsor and Eton (FAC 1)**	H	7-2	3,087	Beasant	Jones	Armstrong	Galliers	Smith 2	Cunningham 1	Ketteridge	Hodges	Leslie	Cork 1	Hubbick 3	Denny
29	Bury	A	0-1	2,392	Beasant	Jones	Armstrong	Galliers	Smith	Cunningham	Ketteridge	Hodges	Leslie	Cork	Hubbick	Denny (3)
Dec. 6	**Darlington**	H	1-1	1,811	Beasant	Brown	Jones	Galliers	Smith	Cunningham	Ketteridge	Denny	Leslie	Cork	Hubbick	Joseph (7) 1
13	**Swindon Town (FAC 2)**	H	2-0	3,470	Beasant	Brown	Jones	Galliers	Smith	Cunningham	Ketteridge	Hodges	Leslie 1	Cork	Denny 1	Hubbick (7)
26	Torquay United	A	3-2	3,191	Beasant	Jones	Armstrong	Galliers	Smith	Cunningham	Ketteridge	Denny	Leslie 1	Cork 1	Hubbick 1	Brown
27	**A.F.C. Bournemouth**	H	2-0	2,681	Beasant	Jones	Armstrong	Galliers	Cunningham	Smith	Ketteridge	Denny	Cork 1	Downes	Hubbick 1	Dziadulewicz
Jan. 3	**Oldham Athletic (FAC 3)**	H	0-0	4,693	Beasant	Jones	Armstrong	Galliers	Smith	Cunningham	Ketteridge	Denny	Leslie	Cork	Hubbick	Downes (5)
6	Oldham Athletic Replay	A	1-0	6,789	Beasant	Jones	Armstrong	Galliers	Smith	Brown	Ketteridge	Denny	Leslie	Cork 1	Hubbick	Hodges (11)
19	**Scunthorpe United**	H	2-2	2,112	Beasant	Jones	Armstrong	Galliers 1	Smith	Brown	Ketteridge	Hodges	Denny	Cork 1	Downes	Hubbick (6)

21	**Halifax Town**	H	3-0	2,501	Beasant	Jones	Armstrong	Galliers 1	Smith	Cunningham	Ketteridge	Hodges	Leslie	Cork 1	Downes 1	Joseph (7)
28	Lincoln City	A	0-0	3,988	Beasant	Jones	Armstrong	Galliers	Smith	Cunningham	Ketteridge	Hodges	Leslie	Cork	Downes	Denny (8)
Mar. 4	Peterborough United	A	1-1	3,201	Beasant	Jones	Armstrong	Galliers	Smith	Cunningham	Ketteridge	Hodges	Leslie	Cork 1	Downes	Denny
7	**Tranmere Rovers**	H	2-1	2,394	Beasant	Jones	Armstrong	Galliers	Smith	Cunningham	Ketteridge	Hodges 1	Leslie 1	Cork	Downes	Hubbick
14	Hartlepool United	A	3-2	2,329	Beasant	Jones	Armstrong	Galliers	Smith	Cunningham	Ketteridge	Hodges	Leslie	Cork 2	Downes 1	Denny (8)
17	Darlington	A	1-4	2,019	Beasant	Jones	Armstrong	Galliers	Smith 1	Cunningham	Ketteridge	Hodges	Leslie	Cork	Downes	Denny
22	**Hereford United**	H	0-0	3,898	Goddard	Jones	Armstrong	Denny	Smith	Downes	Ketteridge	Hodges	Leslie	Cork	Hubbick	Joseph (11)
28	York City	A	1-0	2,026	Goddard	Jones	Armstrong	Denny	Smith	Cunningham	Ketteridge	Hodges	Leslie	Cork 1	Downes	Joseph
31	**Wigan Athletic**	H	1-0	2,638	Goddard	Jones	Armstrong	Denny	Smith	Cunningham	Ketteridge	Hodges 1	Leslie	Cork	Downes	Joseph (8)
Apr. 4	**Doncaster Rovers**	H	1-0	3,595	Goddard	Brown	Armstrong	Denny	Smith	Cunningham	Ketteridge	Hodges	Leslie	Cork 1	Downes	Gage
11	Northampton Town	A	1-1	2,121	Goddard	Brown	Armstrong	Denny	Smith	Cunningham 1	Ketteridge	Belfield	Leslie	Cork	Downes	Joseph (10)
18	A.F.C. Bournemouth	A	1-0	5,048	Goddard	Brown	Armstrong	Galliers	Smith	Cunningham	Ketteridge	Denny	Leslie	Joseph	Downes 1	Belfield
20	**Torquay United**	H	1-0	3,109	Beasant	Jones	Armstrong	Galliers	Smith	Cunningham 1	Ketteridge	Denny	Leslie	Joseph	Downes	Hubbick
25	Wigan Athletic	A	0-1	3,381	Beasant	Brown	Armstrong	Galliers	Smith	Cunningham	Ketteridge	Denny	Leslie	Joseph	Downes	Hodges (3)
28	**Rochdale**	H	4-1	3,884	Beasant	Brown	Jones	Galliers 1	Smith	Cunningham	Ketteridge	Hodges 1	Leslie 2	Denny	Downes	Joseph
May. 2	**Bury**	H	2-4	2,293	Goddard 1	Brown	Downs	Gage	Jones	Cunningham	Ketteridge	Denny 1	Hodges	Joseph	Hubbick	Leslie

FINAL TABLE

LEAGUE DIVISION FOUR

	P	W	D	L	F	A	W	D	L	F	A	Pts
Southend	46	19	4	0	47	6	11	3	9	32	25	67
Lincoln	46	15	7	1	44	11	10	8	5	22	14	65
Doncaster	46	15	4	4	36	20	7	8	8	23	29	56
Wimbledon	46	15	4	4	42	17	8	5	10	22	29	55
Peterboro'	46	11	8	4	37	21	6	10	7	31	33	52
Aldershot	46	12	9	2	28	11	6	5	12	15	30	50
Mansfield	46	13	5	5	36	15	7	4	12	22	29	49
Darlington	46	13	6	4	43	23	6	5	12	22	36	49
Hartlepool	46	14	3	6	42	22	6	6	11	22	39	49
Northampton	46	11	7	5	42	26	7	6	10	23	41	49
Wigan	46	13	4	6	29	16	5	7	11	22	39	47
Bury	46	10	8	5	38	21	7	3	13	32	41	45
Bournemouth	46	9	8	6	30	21	7	5	11	17	27	45
Bradford	46	9	9	5	30	24	5	7	11	23	36	44
Rochdale	46	11	6	6	33	25	3	9	11	27	45	43
Scunthorpe	46	8	12	3	40	31	3	8	12	20	38	42
Torquay	46	13	2	8	38	26	5	3	15	17	37	41
Crewe	46	10	7	6	28	20	3	7	13	20	41	40
Port Vale	46	10	8	5	40	23	2	7	14	17	47	39
Stockport	46	10	5	8	29	25	6	2	15	15	32	39
Tranmere	46	12	5	6	41	24	1	5	17	18	49	36
Hereford	46	8	8	7	29	20	3	5	15	9	42	35
Halifax	46	9	3	11	28	32	2	9	12	16	39	34
York	46	10	2	11	31	23	2	7	14	16	43	33

GOALS AND GAMES

APPEARANCES AND GOALSCORERS

	Appearances			Goals	
	Lge	Cup	Sub	Lge	Cup
Gary Armstrong	35	6			
Dave Beasant	34	5			
Micky Belfield	1				
Peter Brown	26	4	2		
Alan Cork	41	9		23	3
Tommy Cunningham	43	8		4	2
Roy Davies	6	1	3		
Paul Denny	21	5	5	1	3
Wally Downes	34	5		4	1
Phil Driver	4	2	1	2	
Kevin Gage	1				
Steve Galliers	37	9		4	
Ray Goddard	12	4		1	
Glyn Hodges	27	3		5	
Dave Hubbick	20	3	2	4	3
Steve Jones	24	7	1		
Francis Joseph	4		7	1	
Steve Ketteridge	38	7	1	1	
John Leslie	43	9	1	11	4
Steve Perkins	11	2			
Mick Smith	44	9	1	2	2

Wimbledon FC 1980-81. Back row: Wally Downes, Ray Goddard, Tommy Cunningham, Mick Smith, Dave Beasant, Steve Jones, Alan Cork, Paul Denny, Steve Ketteridge, Glyn Hodges. Front row: Dario Gradi, Steve Perkins, John Leslie, Roy Davies, Steve Galliers, Gary Armstrong, Peter Brown, Dave Hubbick.

ABOVE: John Leslie has this effort disallowed for offside during the 0-0 draw at Aldershot in the League Cup. BELOW: Francis Joseph forces the ball home from close range for the Dons' goal at home to Millwall.

PARTNERS IN ADVERSITY 1981-82

A poor beginning

Given the pressures of the previous twelve months it was hardly surprising that Wimbledon experienced such a poor season in 1981-82. With the benefit of hindsight, it is clear that it would have been better if the Club had not been promoted in May 1980. Such was the upheaval, a period of consolidation was needed and Third Division football proved too much. Never out of the bottom four the Dons were eventually relegated.

The Hammam-Bassett partnership, which was to bring such glory, took a full twelve months to knock the Club into shape. It was only in the final matches that there were signs of the stunning successes to come. But six wins in the final eight matches proved too little, too late.

Sam Hammam had become the majority shareholder in the Club during the summer of 1981. At that stage the destiny of the Dons was controlled by the directors of Crystal Palace. They obviously had dual interests and were not working solely for the good of Wimbledon. Sam, who had been a Wimbledon director for some time, bought them out. Financially, if offered him nothing, but his love for the Club was already running deep.

Dave Bassett, writing in one of his programme columns, stressed the importance of Hammam. 'Sam only visits England for about 4-6 weeks maximum during any one year and it is impossible for him to run the Club as most majority shareholders do. His love of Wimbledon and his desire for us to have our own identity became so intense that he took a decision which most normal businessmen would not have done. Had he not taken that decision Wimbledon Football Club, in my opinion, would have very quickly ceased to exist.'

The only pre-season additions to the playing squad were Dean Thomas and Bobby Gould. Thomas, a left back, was signed for £4,000 from Nuneaton Boro', while Gould came on a free transfer at the end of a nomadic playing career. Although he never played for the first team and was soon released, Bobby Gould returned six summers later as manager. Succeeding Bassett, he led the Dons to their finest triumph — at Wembley in May 1988.

Three points for a win was introduced for the first time in 1981-82 and Wimbledon reverted to playing in blue. The new strip — blue with yellow trim — was particularly welcomed by supporters, who had disliked the experiments with white and then yellow shirts in previous seasons. Paul Denny and Ray Goddard left the Club during the close season. Goddard rejoined Allen Batsford at Wealdstone, where both men were to enjoy further success.

After 'friendly' games against QPR at home (lost 4-1) and Slough Town away (won 3-1), the Dons were involved in a new tournament — the Group Cup. Its later manifestations included titles like the 'Associate Members Cup' and the 'Freight Rover Trophy' and ended in a final at Wembley. Its inaugural year was more humble: thirty-two teams in eight groups — the winners of each group entering a knock-out section with the final on a League ground.

The Dons were in Group G and, while many teams treated the ties as glorified friendlies, Wimbledon took them seriously and won all three games, finishing top of the Group. Gillingham left Plough Lane having been beaten 4-0, and visits to Orient and Southend yielded two more wins — by 1-0 and 2-1 respectively. It was a promising beginning and augured well for the months ahead.

So it was with a degree of confidence that Wimbledon opened their Division Three campaign at the County Ground, Swindon. A 4-1 defeat appeared to be a nightmare start but the Dons forced 13 corners to Swindon's five, hit the woodwork twice, and continued to create chances until the end. 'The scoreline says we've been stuffed,' said Bassett, 'but it was nothing like that really,' while Swindon boss, John Trollope, was still more complimentary, commenting: 'On another day they might have beaten us'.

The defensive fraility which was to cost the Dons dear all season was already in evidence. The first nine League games produced only two points, from two draws, and 22 goals were conceded. Following the Swindon match the Dons travelled west again, to secure a 0-0 draw in a League Cup 1st Round, first leg match at Aldershot.

The first home League game produced the largest gate for two years — 5,102 — as Wimbledon slumped to a 3-1 defeat by Millwall. Despite a Francis Joseph equaliser midway through the second half, the Lions roared home, leaving Bassett fuming. 'We deservedly got back into the game and then gave it away. Time is running out for some of the players unless they quickly prove they can do it.'

The first point of the season was gained in the next match at Huddersfield, where John Leslie fired home a Gary Armstrong cross 10 minutes into the second half. Town full back Brown deservedly equalised before the end. The 2nd leg of the League Cup-tie with Aldershot in midweek proved third tie lucky — for the Shots. Having knocked them out at this stage in the previous two seasons, Wimbledon expected to progress, but were beaten 3-1 on the night. The third came in the last minute, when ex-Don Malcolm Crosby fired home a free kick from the halfway line!

Another disastrous Plough Lane game followed, with Doncaster Rovers leaving with all three points. Most disappointed man was Alan Cork, who missed a penalty with the score at 0-0. Minutes after Rovers had sealed their win, with a penalty, Cork took a swipe at Richard Dawson and was sent off. It was four successive home defeats only four days later as an impressive Fulham side put three past Dave Beasant, with only John Leslie replying. A sizeable visiting contingent took the crowd over five and a half thousand.

The agony continued at Walsall, where Alan Cork broke his leg after colliding with home 'keeper Ron Green in the 72nd minute. No stretcher could be found and so he was put on the touchline to lie and wait. One eventually turned up but not before Don Penn had scored the winner for the Saddlers. It was the end of the season for Cork, who did not return for over nineteen months. The injury allowed Dave Hubbick his first appearance of the season as the Dons travelled to Bristol Rovers. He took his chance, scoring both goals in a 2-2 draw. But another home defeat followed, this time against Gillingham. The parallels with the Doncaster match were uncanny as Wimbledon again had a man sent off and missed a penalty while their opponents scored from theirs. Quiet man Steve Ketteridge was dismissed in the 81st minute. He was booked by the referee for swearing after being prevented from taking a quick throw. 'As he was writing my name,' said Ketteridge, 'I asked him to look at his linesman. Without another word he pointed to the tunnel and told me to get off'. Glyn Hodges hit the bar after two minutes in a bright opening but he missed a 30th minute penalty. By then Ritchie Bowman had scored from 25 yards, following a mistake from on-loan defender Terry Boyle, making his debut. The Gills wrapped it up near the end.

The gloom deepened at Lincoln's Sincil Bank on 10 October. Suicidal defending left the Dons defeated 5-1 and rooted to the bottom of the table without a win. Manager Bassett described all of their goals as 'defensive nightmares'. The sole reply came from John Leslie in the 37th minute. One bright spark was a promising debut from 19-year-old Paul Lazarus, a free transfer signing from Charlton Athletic.

The financial situation off the pitch was almost as gloomy as the scene upon it. A Board meeting on the Thursday before the Lincoln match confirmed the fans' worst fears. Popular midfielder Steve Galliers was to be allowed to join Noades and Gradi at Palace. The transfer was eventually delayed for ten days, so that Kevin Gage could return to replace him after Youth World Cup duty for England in Australia.

The sale of Galliers for £70,000 was in addition to Tommy Cunningham leaving to join Orient for £40,000 back in September. The two transfers drastically reduced the interest payments on a large bank overdraft. The annual cost was now down to around £7,000.

'That's a far better figure,' explained Bassett, now clearly far more than simply manager of the football side of the Club. 'We feel for our loyal 2,000 or so fans who see us keep selling, but at the end of the day who picks up the chitty?'

'Forget the gates Millwall and Fulham might attract,' he continued. 'We have to do our sums on the Doncaster and Gillinghams that come here. We can't live on those attendances of 2,300 or 2,500. A football club now has three choices for survival — try and live on your gates; put yourself in hock, develop alternative fund raisers. That's where our future lies. By building up the lotteries, the nightclub and the pubs, we can compensate for have 2,500 gates. It will all take time, but if I get bombed out in two or three years, I will be leaving Wimbledon in a better position than when I took over.' He certainly kept his word; when he left six years later, the Dons were in 6th place — in Division One!

ABOVE: Dave Hubbick fires home his second of the night as Wimbledon draw 2-2 at Bristol Rovers' Eastville Stadium. BELOW: Glyn Hodges shoots before David Carr can tackle him in the 5-1 defeat at Lincoln.

From crisis to crisis

With the club at a low ebb, only 1,659 turned up on 17 October for the home game with Chester, who were also without a win. Thirty-three-year-old Peter Suddaby, on loan from Blackpool, made his debut and added stability to a shaky defence. At the other end, Paul Lazarus' first goal for the Club, firing home Terry Boyle's mis-hit shot, ensured the Dons' first-ever three point haul. The team were off the bottom and they celebrated just days later by defeating Plymouth 2-1 after a last gasp strike by Boyle. At the end, relieved fans applauded the win and gave Steve Galliers a rousing send-off before his move to Palace.

The new penalty taker — Peter Brown — made his mark in the next game at Reading. His spot kick came in the 80th minute, but could not prevent a 2-1 defeat. So manager Dave Bassett continued to ring the changes and gave debuts to Mark Morris and Dave Clement at home to Exeter. Morris was fresh from the youth team while the experienced Clement had played many times for England at right back. Bassett had to be content with a 1-1 draw, commenting: 'Having been on top for the first half we got sloppy and let Exeter back into it'.

The side which took the field againt Exeter was transformed from the one which opened the season. Dave Beasant was still in goal; his full backs were now Dave Clement and Peter Brown with Mark Morris and Mick Smith in the centre. Kevin Gage, Steve Ketteridge and Wally Downes controlled the midfield with John Leslie, Paul Lazarus and Francis Joseph up front. New-look Wimbledon took to the road again with successive vists to Portsmouth and Burnley. At Fratton Park future England international Neil Webb scored the only goal for the homesters, while Dave Clement's brilliant free kick at Turf Moore helped the Dons to a 2-2 draw.

Tommy Docherty's Preston side were next at Plough Lane. It was an afternoon of errors, the slip-a-minute football ending with two sending-offs, three bookings, a missed penalty . . . and a beautifully struck winner from substitute Mick Belfield. Dons fans' nerves were on edge until the end as Preston's Bruce missed an 84th minute penalty and the home side ran out 3-2 winners.

The Saturday after was a nostalgic affair. An FA Cup trip to the Eyrie in Bedford brought back memories of Southern League triumphs. Goals from Suddaby and Ketteridge saw the Dons home in what proved to be the Bedfordshire club's last season before folding. Defeat at Chesterfield in their return to League action saw the team return to the bottom once more. The match was not without controversy, as everyone in the ground saw Wally Downes' second-half shot hit the stanchion before rebounding back into play. The referee waved play on to the fury of the Wimbledon team, who eventually went down 2-0.

Another debut boy — 18-year-old Paul Fishenden — came in due to an injury crisis at home to Newport County. After an hour the Welsh team were 3-0 up and seemingly cruising home, but a storming finish brought goals for Clement and Lazarus. It was not enough and, despite having to kick two shots off the line and relying on the heroics of goalkeeper Mark Kendall, Newport held on.

Surely it could not get any worse — but it did. In what proved to be the last game of 1980. Wimbledon were once again dumped out of the FA Cup at Enfield — this time by four goals to one. Enfield boss Eddie McCluskey clearly fancied his chances before the tie. 'We shall be really confident,' he said, 'because Wimbledon are nothing special.'

He was proved right as the Alliance Premier side knocked out the Dons with a resounding second-half display. Despite leading after seven minutes through Peter Brown's penalty, the men from Plough Lane were swept aside with four goals in the last hour.

Only one game escaped the freak weather conditions over the next month — Bristol City away, on 2 January. The Dons' first away win of the season lifted the team off the bottom and made it a happy new year. Francis Joseph was the star; he made two, might have finished on a hat-trick and led Wimbledon in dominating the second half.

Continued bad weather meant it was three weeks before Swindon became the next opponents at Plough Lane. Another new face — Joe Blochel — was in the side but, having gone back to the bottom due to their own inaction, the Dons could only manage a point in a 1-1 draw.

Dave Clement's final game for Wimbledon came at Doncaster. He was stretchered off with a broken leg with eight minutes to go to dampen the celebrations over a 3-1 win. John Leslie scored twice and Blochel scored his first goal for the Club. 'Leslie's best game for over a year,' beamed Bassett adding, 'about time'. He went on: 'Beasant was tremendous when we were under pressure for the first 10 minutes. We were a bit lucky and might have been 3-0 down. But we clawed our way back and showed character to get ourselves going'.

Wins over Peterborough in the Group Cup by 1-0 and Huddersfield in the League by 2-0 meant Dave Bassett could celebrate the anniversary of his appointment as manager. Reflecting back over the year in his programme notes he felt he had 'experienced almost everything that a manager could expect to encounter during any managerial period'.

Even he had not faced death. The same programme included a player profile of Dave Clement, which commiserated with him over his broken leg. Two months later, possibly unable to face the fact that his successful player career was now over, he took his life, an incident which shocked and saddened everyone at the Club. In a season of many lows this was the nadir.

ABOVE: Francis Joseph runs at the Reading defence. A cheerful Lawrie Sanchez looks on. OPPOSITE: Wimbledon, in the shape of Clement, Joseph, Downes, Ketteridge and Gage wait for the referee to push back the Burnley wall at Turf Moor. BELOW: John Leslie scores his first goal from close range in the 3-2 defeat of Preston North End.

ABOVE: Some consolation in the 6-1 defeat at Gillingham as Steve Ketteridge scores from the spot. A young Steve Bruce is on the extreme left. BELOW: Paul Lazarus watches his volley saved by Lincoln goalkeeper David Felgate.

Continuing gloom

With half the season still to go the Dons appeared to be moving in the right direction. Although still bottom, Wimbledon were now only one win away from moving out of the bottom four. Since they had at least one game in hand on all the teams above them, there was an air of optimism around Plough Lane. But football is a cruel game and a run of poor results soon dashed any revival hopes.

The first visit to Craven Cottage for 50 years ended in a 4-1 defeat, as promotion-chasing Fulham scored three times in the last fifteen minutes. For 75 minutes they had matched the Cottagers, indeed for the first 20 minutes of the second half they were so much on top it was embarrassing. But after the second goal, the defence caved in completely.

Worse was to follow as Wimbledon slumped to the heaviest defeat of their short Football League career. The Priestfield Stadium, Gillingham was the venue and once again the defence wilted under sustained pressure. The Kent side scored six times, with only one reply from Paul Lazarus. To complete a gloomy afternoon, bookings for Joseph and Lazarus took the Dons over 200 points — the FA's limit before a disciplinary hearing became mandatory.

The Group Cup provided a respite from the struggle for League points. The semi-final brought under-strength Burnley to Plough Lane. They returned to Lancashire on the wrong end of a 5-0 scoreline. Buoyed up by this, the next visitors, mid-table Bristol Rovers, were beaten at Plough Lane in a match in which Mick Smith starred. In the first half he kicked a Kelly shot off the line with Beasant beaten. Then he moved forward to loop home a 73rd minute header from a Wally Downes free kick.

The two wins raised the hopes of all Dons fans, but there was more disappointment in midweek at the Den. A disputed penalty two minutes from time saw the Lions home by two goals to one. However, Paul Fishenden provided hope for the future by giving his side the lead in only his second full game.

The next three games were all at home and all ended in draws. A stunning strike from young Kevin Gage ensured a point against Lincoln City. Visits to Chester and Plymouth should have followed but a 'flu epidemic, which left nine of the team in bed, caused their postponement. With the virus abating, an exhibition match with Moscow Dynamo produced a thrilling 2-2 draw but the 1,634 crowd was a real disappointment.

Fully fit again, the Dons faced Reading but missed a hatful of chances and had to settle for a 0-0 draw. Next it was off to Devon to face Exeter; sadly the long trip proved fruitless, although a last minute effort from Hodges nearly made the score 2-2. Stewart Evans and Mark Elliott both made full debuts in a re-jigged attack.

With nine points now separating the Dons from the safety of twentieth position, under 2,000 turned up for the visit of Southend. Stewart Evans marked his home debut with a goal in a 3-0 win, which lifted the team off the bottom again. The goal of the night was a superb left foot drive from Francis Joseph, which sealed the victory.

The Dons needed to build on the confidence supplied by their best win of the season in their next game at home to Burnley. But although they had chances — most notably when Alan Stevenson saved Steve Ketteridge's 34th minute spot kick — they could not break down the Lancastrian defence. The 0—0 draw was a nightmare for Dave Bassett. 'I dreamt on Friday night we would win 1-0 through a penalty', he said. 'I don't know why Ketteridge took it. Peter Brown is our penalty taker. We showed a lot of character again. Burnley took the first half hour, but we were on top from then.'

The news of Dave Clement's death reached the team on the afternoon of their trip to Chester. The result was a supercharged atmosphere when the Dons took to the field. The players were easily upset by some of the early Chester tackling, a match between the two bottom teams. Wimbledon responded in kind and ended with nine men — Peter Brown and Wally Downes were ordered off for violent conduct — and four more were booked. Despite being two players short, the Dons fought back with a Francis Joseph shot, ensuring a 1-1 draw.

Despite a wonderful long-range lob from John Leslie, Wimbledon lost their next match — 3-2 at Preston — before travelling to Grimsby Town for the Group Cup Final. Once again the Dons lost 3-2 but what a match it was. Two-nil down after half an hour, Mark Elliott's first goal for the Club was followed by a Mick Smith equaliser. Only 15 minutes remained when Tony Ford scored the winner for the home team. It left Wimbledon and their vocal support nothing to savour, but glory in defeat.

For the fourth successive game the Dons had to travel, this time for an 11.30 kick-off at Southend on Good Friday. A lethargic performance produced a 2-0 defeat. Back home on Easter Monday there was no good news as local rivals Brentford inflicted a 2-1 defeat. Dave Bassett admitted: 'It's looking grim, very grim. We played like a team lacking confidence; frightened in case we lost. You've got to have bottle in these situations, but we didn't'. The Dons were now seven points from safety with only Chester below them.

The fortunes of Plymouth Argyle had been transformed since their visit to SW19 in the autumn. A 2-0 win over Wimbledon at Home Park in the week after Easter took them into sixth place. For the Dons it was another grim evening. Three days later Wimbledon went west again to visit Newport County. Little football was possible in the strong wind and the team returned to South London, having settled for a 0-0 draw.

The visit of Oxford United led to a five goal thriller with the lead changing hands before the Dons finally lost 3-2. An own goal 17 minutes from time all but condemned Wimbledon to another spell in Division Four. John Leslie, playing as a make-shift right back because of injuries and suspensions, steered the ball past the stranded Dave Beasant. Manager Dave Bassett remained defiant but admitted: 'It now looks distinctly unlikely that we shall avoid the drop, but we shall be fighting like mad to ensure we gain the maximum points available'.

With only eight games left the bottom of the table looked like this:

	P	W	D	L	F	A	Pts
19 Doncaster	40	12	12	16	56	60	48
20 Newport	39	11	14	14	33	48	47
21 Swindon	39	10	12	17	46	62	42
22 Bristol City	38	8	10	24	27	54	34
23 Wimbledon	38	8	10	20	43	67	34
24 Chester	38	7	10	21	34	65	31

Thirteen points from the safety of twentieth place it all looked lost.

LEFT: Wally Downes clears as a youthful Lawrie Sanchez arrives too late to maintain this Reading attack. RIGHT: Mick Smith heads home a free kick from Steve Ketteridge in the 3-0 home win over Southend. BELOW: Mark Elliott is brought down on the edge of the area as the Dons try to find a way past the Burnley defence.

ABOVE: Micky Belfield (hidden) sticks out a foot to score the Dons' second goal against Chesterfield. BELOW: With the Walsall defence beaten, Francis Joseph just fails to make contact with this Dean Thomas cross.

A remarkable late run

Wimbledon, buffeted by financial insecurity and inconsistent performances, suddenly had cause to smile again. A late run with a young side brimming with enthusiasm took them to the brink of safety. Off the field too there was good news, with rumours that the restrictive pre-emption clause might be lifted.

One of the directors, Quentin Spicer, explained what the clause meant for the Club. 'Basically it means that the Local Authority has the right to take back the ground for approximately the sum of £8,000 if at any time we ceased playing football here. The condition was imposed in 1959 when the ground was bought for the Club by the late Sydney Black, the then Chairman. At that time, with an amateur team and no inflation, £8,000 was a lot of money.

'The effect of the pre-emption figure, apart from that produced by inflation, is that any value which we have added to the ground such as Nelsons Nightclub or extending the North Stand, does not increase the buy-out figure. The organisations who might otherwise have considered putting in significant sums to build income producing facilities have been deferred because, if at the worst the Club failed, then the Local Authority could take back the ground plus the facilities all for £8,000.

'A similar situation arises on the Club itself wishing to borrow money to spend on the ground. A Bank would always look at the sale price in the worse circumstances and lend a proportion of that, ie, less than £8,000. The present working overdraft is secured principally by the personal guarantee of directors and senior management.'

Although it took another year for the deal to go through, having the pre-emption lifted gave Wimbledon the chance to back their ambitious plans financially. On the pitch Dave Bassett and his players were responsible for the remarkable success that followed and it was also crucial that the Club was well organised and shrewd off the field. The guidance of Sam Hammam, now with greater leeway fiscally, ensured that.

The final eight games began with the visit of Chesterfield. It was the start of a remarkable run, which took the Dons to the brink of safety. In the end only goal difference sent them down. The Derbyshire side arrived with an outside chance of promotion but left with their hopes in tatters after a 3-1 defeat. After a poor first half, in which only a Micky Belfield goal separated the teams, Wimbledon stepped up the pressure in the second half. Another goal from Belfield and an excellent Glyn Hodges volley secured the points. Unlucky John Leslie had a goal disallowed on his 200th League appearace — the first Don to reach that figure.

Forty-eight hours later, it was onto Griffin Park to face a Brentford side who had beaten the Dons just two weeks before. Two down in 36 minutes the visitors fought back to earn a famous victory. Francis Joseph led the charge with two goals, in a performance of the highest calibre. Since mid-March, when moved to a central 'strikers' role, he had been in brilliant form and scored 11 goals in the last 18 games.

The next match was the visit to League leaders Carlisle, which looked daunting. However, it was Wimbledon who took the lead when home goalkeeper Trevor Swinburne dived over Hodges' 25 yard shot. A penalty in the 57th minute and an unlucky own goal with 15 minutes left led to an unlucky defeat.

Returning to London the Dons faced five games in fourteen days — including four at Plough Lane. For the first match only 1,503 turned up to see a deflected Gary

Armstrong shot and a Stewart Evans tap-in beat Walsall. Already relegated Bristol City were the next visitors and returned west with a point after a 0-0 draw. Manager Bassett was furious with the performance and hauled the side in for extra training on the Sunday. John Leslie was once again unlucky enough to have a goal disallowed, his 67th minute volley ruled out because Evans was in an offside position. Had the goal stood and Wimbledon won, relegation would have been avoided.

Francis Joseph starred once again in the return against a Carlisle side destined for Division Two. Russell Coughlin had just equalised Stewart Evans' first half goal when the 21-year-old took charge. With a draw meaning relegation, he put the Dons back in front with a header from Hodges' 71st minute corner. Four minutes later he latched onto a Beasant clearance, racing clear before calmly slotting home.

In Oxford on the final Saturday of the season three late goals ensured another win. Roy Burton, in the home goal, could not hold Joseph's 74th minute shot and winger Mark Elliott tapped the ball in. Wimbledon struck again in the 81st minute when Joseph's right foot shot from the edge of the box and hit the net. A late penalty from Peter Brown wrapped it up after Elliott's mazy dribble was brought to an abrupt end.

Despite that win only an 11 goal victory would be enough in the final match against Portsmouth on the Tuesday night. Mark Morris's first-ever goal for the Club had the fans singing *Staying Up* but it was never a realistic hope. Pompey equalised before half time and, although an exciting second half saw the Dons home 3-2, they had to accept the agony of a return to Division Four on goal difference.

Manager Dave Bassett was not downhearted. 'We'll be doing all in our power to get straight back up to Division Three,' he said. He was disappointed by the level of support for his side, however, and commented: 'There's no reason to think that we'd get more support even if we were at the top of the Third Division'. His words were to be proved true within eighteen months.

Gary Armstrong heads powerfully towards the Walsall goal.

ABOVE: The 'goal' that would have kept the Dons up! John Leslie is fractionally offside as he fires home in the 0-0 draw with Bristol City. BELOW: Alan Cork hits the rebound from the penalty, but once again Doncaster 'keeper Willie Boyd saves.

ABOVE: John Leslie harries a Doncaster defender during the home defeat. BELOW: Kevin Gage fails to make contact but Peter Suddaby (centre) stoops to head the first goal at the Eyrie.

Memorable Matches 1981-82

19 September 1918: FOOTBALL LEAGUE DIVISION THREE
Wimbledon 0
Doncaster Rovers 1 *Warboys*

The bad blood that existed between these teams exploded in the tunnel at the end of a match which included two sending-offs, two penalties and a booking. The incident occurred when Doncaster players approached the home dressing room, baiting a Wimbledon opponent. Doncaster's Richard Dawson ended up with a broken nose and claimed he had been punched.

Doncaster manager Billy Bremner appeared ready to forget the incident once he had herded his players away under police protection three hours after the final whistle. But Doncaster secretary Roger Reade said: 'The manager and directors will be meeting this week to decide the course of action. We don't want to make a major incident out of this, but it was unsavoury and we are considering various actions'. And Reade finished: 'Dawson is deciding whether to bring charges himself'.

The previous season at Belle Vue, Wimbledon had lost a controversial encounter 2-1. The Dons directors were verbally taunted throughout by home supporters and had beer thrown over them. Director Doug Miller's son Paul, later to play for the Club, was hit by a missile and the referee needed police protection off the pitch.

That was the background to a miserable afternoon for Wimbledon, particularly Alan Cork. Floored in the area by Hugh Dowd's 28th minute challenge, Willie Boyd dived to block Cork's penalty and then won the race for the rebound.

Cork's agony was complete three minutes from time, when he was sent off by referee Mike Taylor for taking a swipe at Dawson. Doncaster substitute Ian Nimmo followed, after fighting with Steve Galliers in an off-the-ball incident in the last seconds. Nimmo had been on for just seven minutes.

The fiery finish was sparked by an 80th minute penalty. Doncaster's Billy Russell followed in on Dave Beasant after he had gathered the ball, he responded by aiming a kick at the player and a penalty ensued. Alan Warboys converted from the spot to seal a 1-0 win for the Yorkshiremen.

'That penalty probably did it all,' said Bassett. 'It fired different sorts of emotions.' A Monday morning telephone call between the two managers closed the incident and the meeting in Yorkshire later in the season passed off without problems.

Wimbledon's young side were in the middle of a disastrous start to the season. Inexperienced and over-enthusiastic they were easy prey for wily opponents. They lost their opening five games at Plough Lane, including a League Cup-tie with Aldershot, and found themselves bottom of the table.

Disappointed boss Dave Bassett warned: 'Time is running out for some players unless they quickly prove they can still do it'. In truth his options were limited. He had to sell players to raise money to pay off debts and he knew in his heart that his team needed strengthening. When leading scorer Alan Cork broke his leg the following week at Walsall, he must have felt the whole world was against him.

WIMBLEDON: Beasant, Jones, Armstrong, Galliers, Smith, Downes, Ketteridge, Gage, Leslie, Cork, Hodges. Sub: Hubbick.
DONCASTER ROVERS: Boyd, Russell, Dawson, Snodin, I., Lally (Nimmo), Dowd, Pugh, Harle, Warboys, Lister, Douglas.
CROWD: 2,364 REFEREE: Mr M. Taylor (Dover)

21 November 1981: FA Cup 1st ROUND
Bedford Town 0
Wimbledon 2 *Suddaby, Ketteridge*

After 73 years this proved to be the last FA Cup-tie played by the Eagles of Bedford at their Eyrie. It was fitting that Wimbledon, regular visitors to the ground for Southern League encounters in the 1960s and 1970s, should be their final Cup opponents.

Having convincingly brushed aside Hoddesdon, Ely, Barton, Potter and Wisbech in the qualifying rounds, the 3,900 crowd were hoping for a Football League scalp. The bumper attendance helped the Club survive for a few more months but, by the summer of 1982, their debts forced them to close.

The Dons showed little mercy on the pitch, calmly and clinically finishing off the Southern League side with little apparent bother. Although Bedford could point to injuries to player-manager Trevor Gould and Graham Felton, which reduced them to ten men for much of the second half, in truth they were beaten long before then.

Wimbledon bettered Bedford in every area including commitment. Many a Cup giant-killing has been caused by battling, hard-working displays but the Dons were quicker to every loose ball and fiercer in the tackle.

Peter Suddaby, playing only his second game for the Dons while on loan, opened the scoring after just six minutes. He was left unmarked at the far post from Micky Belfield's corner and stooped low to head home.

Although giant striker Cliff Campbell was just wide with a header, Wimbledon continued to dominate. Steve Ketteridge and John Leslie both went close before Leslie touched home Paul Lazarus' cross, only for the 'goal' to be disallowed for offside.

Trevor Gould, brother of Bobby, was stretchered off after Peter Brown's crunching tackle in the 22nd minute. He was the sole survivor from the last meeting between the teams in the spring of 1977, when a 2-0 win helped the Dons to their third consecutive Southern League title and a place in the Football League.

The Bedford side were in real trouble when Felton suffered badly bruised ribs shortly before half time. Felton continued, in some pain, until the 74th minute, before he finally left the field leaving his side down to ten men.

Wimbledon had secured the tie by then. Paul Lazarus' 47th minute cross had caused panic as Leslie challenged goalkeeper Tony Luff. The ball ran slowly along the goal line, allowing Steve Ketteridge the simple task of running it home.

There was little further action as Wimbledon did enough to ensure their name was in the hat for the 2nd Round draw. The following Monday the Dons learned that their opponents in the next round would be Enfield, their conquerors in 1977. Bassett was bullish when he heard the news. 'I want Wimbledon in the third round and we're not going to let Enfield stand in our way. We applied ourselves in the right manner at Bedford and Enfield will get the same treatment.'

Brave words, but a 4-1 defeat at Southbury Road ended Wimbledon's hopes for another year. For the Dons there would be another year, for Bedford fans only memories.

BEDFORD TOWN: Luff, Platnaeur, James, Gould (Kirkup), Goodeve, Best, Kurila, McGowan, Robinson, Campbell, Felton.
WIMBLEDON: Beasant, Clement, Brown, Gage, Morris, Suddaby, Ketteridge (Hodges), Leslie, Lazarus, Downes, Belfield.
CROWD: 3,900 REFEREE: Mr A. Hamil (Wolverhampton)

9 February 1982: FOOTBALL LEAGUE DIVISION THREE
Fulham 4 *Coney 2, Downes (o.g.), Wilson*
Wimbledon 1 *Ketteridge*

Wimbledon's first visit to Craven Cottage for over 50 years ended in a heavy defeat, as Fulham struck three times in the last 15 minutes. But for over an hour they had matched the Cottagers, and for the first 20 minutes of the second half they were so on top, it was embarrassing.

'You don't always get what you deserve in life,' summed up Dons boss Dave Bassett. 'We were punished in the end, having played with skill and entertained.' The match turned when Fulham regained the lead in the 75th minute, after Wally Downes deflected a Les Strong free kick into his own net. 'The ball came over and hit me in the face,' said the disconsolate Downes. 'There was nothing I could do.'

It was a cracking local derby from the moment ex-Don Ray Lewington's 25-yard snap-shot grazed the top of the Wimbledon bar in the fifth minute. Francis Joseph replied with a driven cross shot, which Peyton did well to hold before a Peter Brown drive was turned over.

Fulham took the lead, however, when Dave Beasant missed, at full stretch, Kevin Lock's 13th minute cross. Dean Coney arrived at the far post to bury a bullet header. Despite more pressure from the home side, there was no further score before half time; indeed, had Brown and Lazarus taken their chances, Wimbledon might have been on level terms.

Bassett's interval team talk was obviously stirring stuff, for the Dons came out and were immediately on top. The equaliser they deserved came after 55 minutes and it was fitting that the Don's two best players on the night — Downes and Joseph — should set it up. Joseph broke clear down the right and, after a clever one-two with Downes, crossed low for Steve Ketteridge. He turned sharply on the ball and fired home from ten yards.

Centre forward Joe Blochel then wasted three golden chances in 15 minutes as Wimbledon searched for a rare away win. But the Dons failed to take advantage when they had the initiative and the match slipped away from them after the own goal.

Once behind for the second time Wimbledon caved in completely and at times were over-run. Robert Wilson headed the third in off Dave Beasant's hands in the 85th minute and slack marking allowed Dean Coney a free, six-yard drive for the fourth.

With the Dons pushing forward to try to salvage some pride, Fulham's Wilson, Coney, Sean O'Driscoll and Gordon Davies could all have scored in the final 10 minutes.

The shell-shocked Dons travelled on to Gillingham's Priestfield Stadium four days later and were on the wrong end of a 6-1 score line, at that time their record defeat in a Football League match. The result left Wimbledon rooted to the bottom of the table with 23 points from 24 matches.

If Wimbledon appeared naive it was not surprising. The average age of the team was only 20 and Gary Armstrong, at 24, was the oldest. The team were enduring some harsh lessons in an unforgiving world. Luckily for Dons supporters, they were quick learners.

FULHAM: Peyton, Lock, Strong, O'Driscoll, Brown, Gale, Davies, Wilson, Coney, O'Sullivan, Lewington.

WIMBLEDON: Beasant, Brown, Thomas, Smith, Morris, Downes, Ketteridge, Lazarus, Blochel, Armstrong, Joseph. Sub: Hodges (not used).

CROWD: 7,802 REFEREE: Mr K. Baker (Rugby)

26 April 1982: FOOTBALL LEAGUE DIVISION THREE
Brentford 2 *Bowles, Johnson*
Wimbledon 3 *Joseph 2, Belfield*

The famous Wimbledon fighting spirit showed itself in a match where the side appeared beaten after going in 2-0 down at half-time. But with the wind behind them, they stormed back to record a victory against local rivals, who had won at Plough Lane just two weeks earlier.

The first half belonged to Stan Bowles, in the twilight of an illustrious career. He opened the scoring after 11 minutes, from a free kick awarded after Gary Armstrong had brought him down on the edge of the box. He picked himself up to curl the ball over the Dons' wall and beyond the dive of the despairing Beasant.

After 36 minutes it was two-nil. With the wind playing havoc, Beasant had just had to be at his best to hold onto Gary Roberts' swirling cross. He could only watch as Gary Johnson hooked home a volley from 25 yards, which swerved in the wind and dipped under the bar. A rueful Bassett commented later: 'He is unlikely to score another goal like that as long as he lives'.

Having changed ends it was a different story. Within minutes Wimbledon pulled a goal back with the best move of the match. Glyn Hodges received a throw from Dean Thomas on the left wing. He drew Bowles out of position before releasing the overlapping Gary Armstrong. His deep cross was headed back by the lanky Stewart Evans, leaving Francis Joseph with an easy chance.

On the hour the Dons were level. Once again the marauding Armstrong set it up. He burst through three tackles down the left wing, before cutting in and unleashing an 18-yard drive which came back off the bar for Micky Belfield to head home.

With a sizeable visiting contingent urging their favourites to go for the win, the Dons duly obliged. Belfield received a deflection on the edge of the Brentford box and laid the ball off, for Joseph to thump a rising drive beyond the bemused David McKellar in the Bees goal.

Despite late Brentford pressure, Wimbledon somehow held on. Armstrong denied substitute Booker with a last-ditch tackle in the six-yard box, Booker put another chance against the bar and a Jim McNichol blockbuster caught Kevin Gage in the face and bounced to safety.

As manager Bassett so rightly said: 'Our players gave a gritty and determined performance in the second half to get back into the game and earn a thoroughly deserved win'. He also praised the Wimbledon fans. 'Several managers have commented on the loyalty of our fans in their support of the team. In similar circumstances their fans would have been abusing and criticising.'

With six games left, Wimbledon were third bottom, two places but eight points away from safety. Their late surge continued, with four wins and a draw in the remaining matches, but it was not enough to avoid a return to Division Four. Francis Joseph's performance in the match was an important factor in him joining Brentford in the summer of 1982.

BRENTFORD: McKellar, McNichol, Tucker, Salman, Whitehead, Hurlock, Kamara, Johnson, Bowen, Bowles, Robers. Sub: Booker.
WIMBLEDON: Beasant, Leslie, Armstrong, Smith, Morris, Downes, Thomas, Joseph, Hodges, Evans, Belfield. Sub: Gage.
CROWD: 6,612 REFEREE: Mr B. Daniels (Brentwood)

ABOVE: Steve Ketteridge (centre with hair on end) stabs home the second and decisive goal at Bedford. BELOW: Fulham's Gerry Peyton punches clear under pressure from Francis Joseph.

ABOVE: Steve Ketteridge gets the better of Les Strong before scoring the Dons' goal at Craven Cottage. BELOW: Dave Beasant saves at point-blank range from Brentford's Bowen.

The front cover of the programme issued at Griffin Park.

1981 - 82 AT A GLANCE

DATE	OPPONENTS	H/A	Res.	Att.	1	2	3	4	5	6	7	8	9	10	11	12
Aug.15	**Gillingham (GC)**	H	4-0	1,352	Beasant	Brown	Armstrong 1	Galliers	Smith 1	Downes	Fear 1	Joseph	Leslie 1	Cork	Hodges	Ketteridge (11)
18	Orient (GC)	A	1-0	1,777	Beasant	Brown	Armstrong	Galliers	Smith	Cunningham	Ketteridge	Joseph	Leslie	Cork 1	Downes	Hodges (4)
24	Southend United (GC)	A	2-1	1,780	Beasant	Brown	Thomas	Gage	Smith	Jones	Ketteridge	Joseph	Hubbick	Lazarus 2	Hodges	Docker
29	Swindon Town	A	1-4	5,632	Beasant	Brown	Armstrong	Galliers	Smith	Jones	Ketteridge 1	Joseph	Leslie	Cork	Hodges	Gage (11)
Sept. 1	Aldershot (FLC1)	A	0-0	2,098	Beasant	Jones	Armstrong	Galliers	Smith	Downes	Ketteridge	Joseph	Leslie	Cork	Hodges	Brown
5	**Millwall**	H	1-3	5,102	Beasant	Jones	Armstrong	Galliers	Smith	Cunningham	Ketteridge	Joseph 1	Leslie	Cork	Downes	Hodges
12	Huddersfield Town	A	1-1	7,326	Beasant	Jones	Armstrong	Galliers	Smith	Cunningham	Ketteridge	Joseph	Leslie 1	Cork	Downes	Hodges
15	**Aldershot (FLC1)**	H	1-3	2,181	Beasant	Brown	Armstrong	Galliers	Smith	Downes	Ketteridge	Joseph	Leslie	Cork 1	Hodges	Gage (2)
19	**Doncaster Rovers**	H	0-1	2,364	Beasant	Jones	Armstrong	Galliers	Smith	Downes	Ketteridge	Gage	Leslie	Cork	Hodges	Hubbick (7)
22	**Fulham**	H	1-3	5,554	Beasant	Jones	Armstrong	Galliers	Smith	Downes	Ketteridge	Gage	Leslie 1	Cork	Hodges	Hubbick (8)
26	Walsall	A	0-1	3,027	Beasant	Brown	Jones	Galliers	Smith	Downes	Ketteridge	Hodges	Leslie	Cork	Joseph	Gage (10)
29	Bristol Rovers	A	2-2	5,364	Beasant	Brown	Thomas	Galliers	Smith	Jones	Ketteridge	Armstrong	Hubbick 2	Downes	Hodges	Joseph (9)
Oct. 3	**Gillingham**	H	0-2	2,510	Beasant	Jones	Thomas	Galliers	Smith	Boyle	Ketteridge	Hodges	Hubbick	Downes	Armstrong	Lazarus (3)
10	Lincoln City	A	1-5	3,160	Beasant	Jones	Thomas	Galliers	Smith	Boyle	Ketteridge	Hodges	Leslie 1	Downes	Lazarus	Joseph
17	**Chester**	H	1-0	1,659	Beasant	Brown	Jones	Galliers	Smith	Boyle	Leslie	Hodges	Lazarus 1	Downes	Suddaby	Joseph
20	**Plymouth Argyle**	H	2-1	2,114	Beasant	Brown	Jones	Galliers	Smith	Suddaby	Boyle 1	Leslie	Lazarus	Downes	Hodges	Joseph (3) 1
24	Reading	A	1-2	3,732	Beasant	Brown 1	Joseph	Boyle	Smith	Suddaby	Leslie	Ketteridge	Lazarus	Downes	Hodges	Gage (11)
31	**Exeter City**	H	1-1	2,152	Beasant	Clement	Brown	Gage	Smith	Morris	Leslie	Ketteridge	Lazarus 1	Downes	Joseph	Hodges (7)
Nov. 3	Portsmouth	A	0-1	9,063	Beasant	Clement	Brown	Gage	Geddes	Morris	Leslie	Ketteridge	Lazarus	Downes	Joseph	Fishenden (7)
7	Burnley	A	2-2	4,231	Beasant	Clement 1	Brown	Gage	Morris	Geddes	Leslie	Ketteridge	Lazarus 1	Downes	Joseph	Thomas
14	**Preston North End**	H	3-2	2,428	Beasant	Clement	Brown	Gage	Morris	Suddaby	Leslie 2	Ketteridge	Lazarus	Downes	Joseph	Belfield (11) 1
21	Bedford Town (FAC1)	A	2-0	3,900	Beasant	Clement	Brown	Gage	Morris	Suddaby 1	Ketteridge 1	Leslie	Lazarus	Downes	Belfield	Hodges (9)
28	Chesterfield	A	0-2	4,604	Beasant	Clement	Armstrong	Gage	Morris	Suddaby	Brown	Leslie	Hodges	Downes	Joseph	Belfield (4)
Dec. 5	**Newport County**	H	2-3	2,056	Beasant	Clement 1	Armstrong	Fishenden	Morris	Suddaby	Brown	Leslie	Lazarus 1	Downes	Joseph	Bolton
15	Enfield (FAC2)	A	1-4	2,730	Beasant	Clement	Brown 1	Fishenden	Morris	Suddaby	Ketteridge	Leslie	Lazarus	Downes	Joseph	Gage
Jan. 2	Bristol City	A	3-1	4,660	Beasant	Clement	Thomas	Smith	Morris	Downes	Ketteridge 1	Leslie	Lazarus 2	Hodges	Joseph	Brown
23	**Swindon Town**	H	1-1	2,084	Beasant	Clement	Thomas	Smith	Morris	Downes	Ketteridge 1	Leslie	Blochel	Hodges	Joseph	Gage
29	Doncaster Rovers	A	3-1	5,849	Beasant	Clement	Thomas	Smith	Morris	Downes	Ketteridge	Leslie 2	Blochel 1	Hodges	Joseph	Gage (7)
Feb. 3	Peterborough (GC)	A	1-0	1,835	Beasant	Gage 1	Armstrong	Smith	Morris	Downes	Ketteridge	Leslie	Blochel	Hodges	Joseph	Brown (10)
6	**Huddersfield Town**	H	2-0	2,499	Beasant	Brown	Thomas	Smith	Morris	Downes	Ketteridge 2	Leslie	Blochel	Armstrong	Joseph	Lazarus
9	Fulham	A	1-4	7,802	Beasant	Brown	Thomas	Smith	Morris	Downes	Ketteridge 1	Lazarus	Blochel	Armstrong	Joseph	Hodges
13	Gillingham	A	1-6	4,214	Beasant	Brown	Thomas	Smith	Morris	Downes	Ketteridge 1	Lazarus	Blochel	Armstrong	Joseph	Hodges (3)
16	**Burnley (GC)**	H	5-0	1,267	Hatcher	Brown	Thomas	Hodges 1	Morris	Downes	Ketteridge	Lazarus 2	Blochel 1	Armstrong	Joseph 1	Fishenden (2)
20	**Bristol Rovers**	H	1-0	2,408	Beasant	Gage	Armstrong	Smith 1	Morris	Downes	Ketteridge	Lazarus	Blochel	Hodges	Joseph	Elliott
24	Millwall	A	1-2	4,072	Beasant	Gage	Armstrong	Smith	Morris	Brown	Ketteridge	Lazarus	Fishenden 1	Hodges	Joseph	Elliott

Date	Opponent	Venue	Score	Att.	1	2	3	4	5	6	7	8	9	10	11	12
23	**Southend United**	H	3-0	1,951	Beasant	Brown	Armstrong	Smith 1	Morris	Downes	Ketteridge	Joseph 1	Evans 1	Hodges	Elliott	Leslie (10
27	**Burnley**	H	0-0	2,641	Beasant	Brown	Armstrong	Smith	Morris	Downes	Ketteridge	Joseph	Evans	Leslie	Elliott	Belfield (10)
31	Chester	A	1-1	1,359	Beasant	Brown	Armstrong	Smith	Morris	Downes	Ketteridge	Joseph 1	Evans	Leslie	Elliott	Belfield (11)
Apr. 3	Preston North End	A	2-3	4,964	Beasant	Brown 1	Armstrong	Smith	Morris	Downes	Ketteridge	Joseph	Evans	Hodges	Belfield	Leslie (11) 1
6	Grimsby Town (GC)	A	2-3	3,423	Beasant	Brown	Armstrong	Smith 1	Morris	Downes	Ketteridge	Joseph	Lazarus	Hodges	Leslie	Elliott (11) 1
9	Southend United	A	0-2	4,779	Beasant	Brown	Armstrong	Smith	Morris	Downes	Gage	Joseph	Evans	Hodges	Lazarus	Elliott (11)
12	**Brentford**	H	1-2	4,513	Beasant	Brown	Armstrong	Smith	Morris	Downes	Gage	Joseph 1	Evans	Hodges	Elliott	Belfield (7)
14	Plymouth Argyle	A	0-2	4,748	Beasant	Thomas	Armstrong	Smith	Morris	Belfield	Elliott	Hughes	Leslie	Evans	Joseph	Gage (8)
17	Newport County	A	0-0	3,900	Beasant	Thomas	Armstrong	Smith	Morris	Belfield	Hughes	Leslie	Evans	Fishenden	Elliott	Ketteridge (7)
20	**Oxford United**	H	2-3	2,903	Beasant	Leslie	Armstrong	Smith	Morris	Downes	Ketteridge	Joseph 1	Hodges	Evans 1	Belfield	Thomas
24	**Chesterfield**	H	3-1	2,138	Beasant	Leslie	Armstrong	Smith	Morris	Downes	Ketteridge	Joseph	Hodges 1	Evans	Belfield 2	Gage
26	Brentford	A	3-2	6,612	Beasant	Leslie	Armstrong	Smith	Morris	Downes	Thomas	Joseph 2	Hodges	Evans	Belfield 1	Gage
May 1	Carlisle United	A	1-2	4,466	Beasant	Leslie	Armstrong	Smith	Morris	Downes	Thomas	Joseph	Hodges 1	Evans	Belfield	Gage
4	**Walsall**	H	2-0	1,503	Beasant	Leslie	Armstrong	Smith	Morris	Downes	Thomas	Joseph	Hodges	Evans 1	Belfield	Gage
8	**Bristol City**	H	0-0	2,114	Beasant	Leslie	Armstrong	Smith	Morris	Downes	Ketteridge	Joseph	Hodges	Evans	Belfield	Ketteridge (11)
11	**Carlisle United**	H	3-1	2,022	Beasant	Leslie	Gage	Smith	Morris	Downes	Thomas	Joseph 2	Hodges	Evans 1	Ketteridge	Elliott
15	Oxford United	A	3-0	4,319	Beasant	Leslie	Thomas	Brown 1	Morris	Downes	Ketteridge	Joseph 1	Hodges	Evans	Gage	Elliott 1
18	**Portsmouth**	H	3-2	2,642	Beasant	Leslie 1	Thomas	Brown	Morris 1	Downes	Ketteridge	Joseph 1	Hodges	Evans	Gage	Elliott

FINAL TABLE

LEAGUE DIVISION THREE

	P	W	D	L	F	A	W	D	L	F	A	Pts
Burnley	46	13	7	3	37	20	8	10	5	29	25	80
Carlisle	46	17	4	2	44	21	6	7	10	21	29	80
Fulham	46	12	9	2	44	22	9	6	8	33	29	78
Lincoln	46	13	7	3	40	16	8	7	8	26	24	77
Oxford	46	10	8	5	28	18	9	16	8	35	31	71
Gillingham	46	14	5	4	44	26	6	6	11	20	30	71
Southend	46	11	7	5	35	23	7	8	8	28	28	69
Brentford	46	8	6	9	28	22	11	5	7	28	25	68
Milwall	46	12	4	7	36	28	6	9	8	26	34	67
Plymouth	46	12	5	6	37	24	6	6	11	27	32	65
Chesterfield	46	12	4	7	33	27	6	6	11	24	31	64
Reading	46	11	6	6	43	35	6	5	12	24	40	62
Portsmouth	46	11	10	2	33	14	3	9	11	23	37	61
Preston	46	10	7	6	25	22	6	6	11	25	34	61
Bristol Rovers	46	12	4	7	35	28	6	5	12	23	37	61
Newport	46	9	10	4	28	21	5	6	12	26	33	58
Huddersfield	46	10	5	8	38	25	5	7	11	26	34	57
Exeter	46	14	4	5	46	33	2	5	16	25	51	57
Doncaster	46	9	9	5	31	24	4	8	11	24	44	56
Walsall	46	10	7	6	32	23	3	7	13	19	32	53
Wimbledon	46	10	6	7	33	27	4	5	14	28	48	53
Swindon	46	9	5	9	37	36	4	8	11	18	35	52
Bristol City	46	7	6	10	24	29	4	7	12	16	36	46
Chester	46	2	10	11	16	30	5	1	17	20	48	32

GOALS AND GAMES

APPEARANCES AND GOALSCORERS

	Appearances			Goals	
	Lge	Cup	Sub	Lge	Cup
Gary Armstrong	31	2			
Dave Beasant	46	4			
Micky Belfield	9	1	5	4	
Joe Blochel	6			1	
Terry Boyle	5			1	
Peter Brown	27	3		3	1
Dave Clement	9	2		2	
Alan Cork	6	2			1
Tommy Cunningham	2				
Wally Downes	42	4			
Paul Elliott	7		4	1	
Stewart Evans	18			4	
Paul Fishenden	4	1	1	1	
Kevin Gage	15	1		1	
Steve Galliers	11	2			
David Geddes	2				
Glyn Hodges	32	2	2	2	
Dave Hubbick	2		2	2	
Billy Hughes	2				
Steve Jones	11	1			
Francis Joseph	38	3	2	13	
Steve Ketteridge	34	4	2	7	1
Paul Lazarus	17	2	1	6	
John Leslie	34	4	4	9	
Mark Morris	33	2		1	
Mick Smith	39	2		2	
Peter Suddaby	6	2			1
Dean Thomas	18				

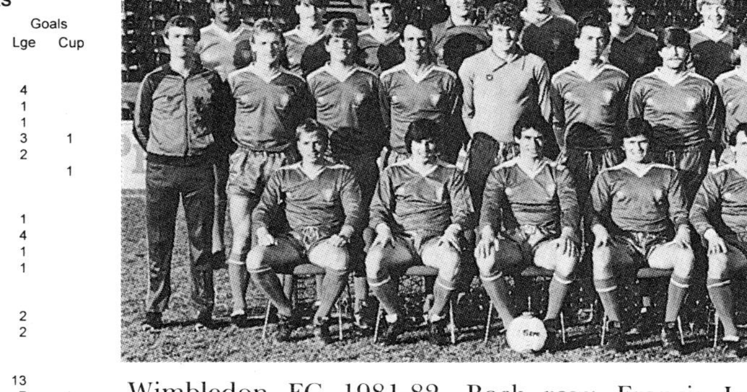

Wimbledon FC 1981-82. Back row: Francis Joseph, Dean Thomas, Peter Brown, Doug Hatcher, Steve Jones, Paul Lazarus, Wally Downes, Kevin Gage. Middle row: Alan Gillett, Peter Suddaby, Glyn Hodges, Alan Cork, Dave Beasant, Mark Morris, Mick Smith, Paul Fishenden, Dave Bassett. Front row: Gary Armstrong, Mickey Belfield, Dave Clement, Steve Ketteridge, John Leslie.

ABOVE: Wally Downes keeps the pressure on Brentford during the Plough Lane clash in April 1982. BELOW: Wimbledon's first visit to Old Trafford — 2 May 1987. Dennis Wise takes on Arthur Albiston; he later scored the winner.

Postscript

On 18 May 1982 Wimbledon beat Portsmouth 3-2 at Plough Lane in front of under 3,000 fans. The one goal margin of victory was not enough and meant they returned to the Fourth Division on goal difference with little prospect of a quick return. Yet under five years later — 2 May 1987 — the Dons left Old Trafford after their first visit to that illustrious stadium, having just completed a remarkable League 'double' over Manchester United. Dennis Wise's late goal was enough to silence the 31,000 crowd and, one week later as the season ended, the South Londoners found themselves in sixth place — in Division One!

Not only did the Dons reach the top division in record time, they then had the audacity to stay there. As I write this, the Club is completing its tenth year in the top division, and in that time there have been few moments when its status has looked under threat.

So what caused such a transformation? Certainly a host of good players have worn the blue of Wimbledon with distinction over the last fifteen years. Few would deny that men like Beasant, Winterburn, Scales, Hodges, Cork, Sanchez, Barton, Wise, Jones, Thorn, Fashanu and Segers have played a huge part in the success of the Club. Without them nothing would have been achieved.

There is also that unique spirit with which the Dons play. The now famous 'Crazy Gang' style, which is so envied and feared throughout the football world, has carried the team through many battles. Reputations and status mean nothing to a Wimbledon team. They are simply used as a spur for even greater determination and effort.

The media have played their part. Since the Club reached the First Division, there has been a non-stop barrage of abuse and vilification aimed at everyone connected with the Dons. The style of play, the state of the ground, the size of the crowds, the disciplinary record, even the lack of previous success, have all been criticised. It seems that only certain clubs, playing football the 'right' way, should be allowed among the elite. But Wimbledon have always drawn strength from such antagonism. Each match is another opportunity to prove the critics wrong and humble supposed superiors.

Undoubtedly Wimbledon have been blessed with a succession of brilliant managers — Bassett, Gould, Harford and Kinnear. All have contributed to the development of the Club. All have understood the Wimbledon way and the necessity of having to raise money by selling their best players. All kept their side among the front-runners of the English game.

One man has remained a constant factor throughout the years of success. Sam Hammam has fostered the spirit, cajoled the players, driven on the managers and used the wrath of the media to encourage all those employed by the Club. At times he must have felt overwhelmed by the strength and numbers of those who opposed his beloved Dons. Yet, despite offers to take his talents elsewhere, he has remained loyal and his vision and desire remain undimmed. Never out-fought in the transfer market, he has managed to pay the bills off the field and maintain progress on it for nearly two decades now.

'Sam is a very "hands on" owner,' says Joe Kinnear. 'He takes the players horse racing, he takes them to the cinema. He's here every day. Some clubs have board meetings every six weeks, I believe. Sam and I have one every day of our lives, because every day we meet and talk about what we want to do. But it has to be worked at. You have to give it a lot of love and attention.'

The next chaper of this story — the journey from 4th to 1st — I hope to tell another day. It is a tale of a battle against the odds that would not be believed if it happened in the pages of fiction. Yet with Wimbledon the extraordinary is commonplace — it is what makes them such a unique Club!

Sam Hammam — inspiration and 'hands on owner'.

INDEX

All figures in *italics* refer to illustrations.

SUBSCRIBERS

Presentation Copies

1 Wimbledon Football Club
2 Sam Hammam, Owner
3 Paul Willatts
4 Peter Cork
5 Peter Miller
6 David Barnard
7 Reg Davis
8 Allen Batsford
9 Joe Kinnear

10 Stephen Crabtree
11 Clive & Carolyn Birch
12 Robert Cubbage
13 Wendy Spicer
14 Brian R. Halliday
15 Russel Chandler
16 Stuart Hall
17 Gary Fletcher
18 Barbara O'Bee
19 Graham Gove
20 Christopher White
21 Neal Exall
22 Scott Harris
23 Derek Mason
24 Graham Kendall
25-26 Mrs P. Patching
27 B. Hern
28 Ron & Cynthia Balch
29 Kevin Barker
30 Robert James Clapshoe
31 P.J. Bailey
32 Steven Mark Flynn
33 Andy Vanstan
34 Robert Claxton
35 Paul Prothero
36 Steve Poole
37 Clem Richards
38 Edward Elstub
39 Lee Walker
40 Neal Andrew Richardson
41 Nicholas Fernyhough
42 Kevin Paul Fitzpatrick
43 Greg Parker
44 Jonathan Ling
45 Robert E.P. Dunford
46 Stephen Pannell
47 O.G.M. Edwards
48-49 Graeme Hodge
50 David McKnight
51 Nathan Andrews
52 Simon G. Carr
53 Andrew Dellow
54 Kevin Hazelwood
55-56 Mark Halls
57-58 Keith Roberts
59 Paul Greenslade
60 Michael Jay
61 Terence J. Tizzard
62 Richard Sawyer
63 Sharon Coe
64 John Branford
65 Lorraine & Barry Cochman
66 Steve Tyler
67 Leslie C. Brooks
68 Dr J. Costello
69 Graham Alan Yeates
70 Michael Patrick Folkes
71 David Lancaster
72 Len Lancaster
73 Gavin Saddington
74 Harry B. Kelsall
75 Jonathan B. Labrum
76 Mark Knight
77 Nigel Jones
78 Caroline Grace
79 James Lamont
80 Marion Hurrell
81 P. Gosling
82 Ronald Victor Evans
83 Nicy Grant
84-87 Margaret Whisker
88 Peter Hilton
89 Nick Blanchard
90 Michael Anthony Costello
91 Shaun Whiteside
92 Peter Cork
93 Dave James
94 Mark Burton
95 R. Rogawski
96 Malcolm Challis
97 Nigel Smith
98 Trevor Shattock
99 Mark Rea
100 Colin Anthony Reed
101 I.G. Holmes
102 Suresh Tolat
103 Stephen Paul Brewer
104 Peter & Harry Young
105 Michael Lloyd
106 Stephen Ward
107 Dennis J. Beckett
108 R.J.P. Thomas
109 Richard Forster
110 Ian Lemon
111 Patrick Adrian Kelly
112 Alan Percival
113 Tony Umpelby
114 Ben Beaver
115 James Potter
116 Duncan Johnson
117 Garry Clark
118 I.R. McNay
119 Rick Crabtree
120 David & Jane Hart
121 Lew Hart
122 Barry Akid
123 Geof Kebbell
124 Shaun Whiteside
125 Michael Mannion
126 Michael A. Baker
127 John C. Howard
128 David Kenwery
129 N. Le-Faye
130 Tom Hillyer
131 Kevin Hillyer
132 Mark Hillyer
133-134 David Trunks
135 Ken J. Wells
136 Luke Meadowcroft
137 Ian Lowe
138 Richard Ward
139 The Smith Family
140 Sam 'The man who can' Morgan
141 Nicki & Mark Hubble
142 Ted Richardson
143 Fess Parker
144 Ron Tutte
145 Peter & Jill Douglass
146 Brian King
147 Jonathan Crabtree
148 Robin Rance
149 Bernard William Podd
150 Stephen Nuttall
151 John Rogers

152 Nick Delawa
153 Andy Harrison
154 Sue Comper
155 Danny Donovan
156 Keith Slatter
157 Nathan David
158 Gordon Wright
159 Daniele Mandelli
160 Ian Gilbert
161 Peter Burrows
162 Mark David Bunworth
163 Peter Bond
164 Roger Stott
165 Michael Field
166 Kevin Field
167 John Balchin
168 Steven John Nott
169 Mark Satchell
170 Nick Dukes
171 Dennis Lowndes
172 Paul Sparks
173 John Tivers
174 Steve Palmer
175 Michael Stephen Taylor
176 Nick Palmowski
177 Paul Hoadley
178 Nigel Standish
179-180 Rob Dickinson
181 Jim Lowther
182 Robert Smith
183 C.W. Finlay
184 John Banfield
185 Alisdair Kemp
186 J.K. O'Sullivan
187 Ian Weller
188 Ian Lightwood
189 Owen G. Williams
190 Marc D. Williams
191 R.J. Jackson
192 David Bayman
193 Neil Smith
194 K. Pink
195 Brian G. White
196 John A. Harris
197 Geoff Allman
198 L. Burgess
199 John Northcutt
200 Geoffrey Wright
201 Brendan J. Rauwerda
202 Gareth A. Evans
203 Donald Ashwood
204 Raymond Shaw
205 Peter Stevenson
206 Guy Stevenson
207 Richard Faulkner
208 Dean Fisher
209 Roberto Bussinelli-Verona
210 Laurence Lowne
211 Adrian Cook
212 Matteo Tonna
213 Kevin Smith
214 Adrian Gill
215 Suzanne Denné
216 Paul Lapraik
217 Alan Davies
218 L.A. Zammit
219 Kelly Verity Bishop
220 C.W. Finlay
221 Helen Patricia Stevens
222 Richard Stocken
223 Mrs M. O'Donnell
224 Sheila Gould
225 Tom Adams
226 Kenneth J. Peacock
227 Michael McManus
228 Robert Ringsell
229 N. Geldard
230 P. Bailey
231 Jim Leake
Remaining names unlisted.